The Tramways of Lancashire and North Wales

(Networks Edition)

This book, the fifteenth in our regional series, is based on parts of Chapters 2 and 11 of *Great British Tramway Networks* by W. H. Bett and J. C. Gillham published in its fourth edition in 1962 and long out of print. In it we cover a number of contrasting areas, the plains of Cheshire, industrialised South Lancashire, the port of Liverpool, the Wirral Peninsula, the north coast of Wales, then to Pwllheli, beyond Snowdonia.

Liverpool was the terminus of a network of tramways, built to a common gauge, that extended eastwards across South Lancashire for forty miles through Manchester to beyond Rochdale and Stalybridge on the flanks of the Pennine hills. On our journey we leave the train at Crewe and by way of Northwich and Warrington arrive at Atherton, the hub of the tramway which linked the Manchester network to that centred on Liverpool. This was operated by the South Lancashire Company, with routes providing links from Salford, Bolton and Wigan, by way of St. Helens and Prescot, to the Merseyside Metropolis. Following a visit to Southport we continue across the Mersey to Birkenhead, the site of Train's pioneer tramway in 1860, and Wallasey. After Chester we cross the border into Wales, visit Wrexham and then travel back to the sea at Rhyl and Llandudno. The journey concludes some forty miles to the south west at Pwllheli on the coast of Tremadoc Bay.

Crewe

The lowlands to the west of the Pennines formed a natural routeway for roads and later canals. It was, therefore, almost inevitable that the railways which followed would converge at a point in the open countryside where cheap land was available. Here the London and North Western Railway established a locomotive works, and by 1911 Crewe had a population of almost 45,000. Crewe was a 'railway town' although other industries have since developed in the area. Seven tramway schemes were proposed for the town between 1879 and 1904 but none of these came to fruition.

The first scheme, promoted by Frederick Charles Winby of Nottingham, was for the Crewe and District Tramways, under the Tramways Orders Confirmation Act of 1879. This authorised a ¼ mile, three-foot gauge line linking the railway station with the railway works to the west of the town centre. It was never built and seventeen years elapsed before the next proposal was put forward.

In 1896 the Light Railways Act received the Royal Assent, and the Crewe and District Light Railways Order, promoted by the British Electric Traction Company, was the first to be applied for anywhere, for a tramway-type line. At the time it caused considerable controversy as to whether a tramway-type railway could be built under the Act. The original proposal was for a line of 9¾ miles of 3ft.6in. gauge track extending from Church Coppenhall in the north through the town to the station and out along the Nantwich Road to Wistaston Cross Roads, plus two routes to beyond the LNWR works and a branch to Crewe Green. The Nantwich Road extension was withdrawn, but the remaining 7¾ miles was approved by the Light Railway Commissioners in December 1897. Unfortunately the B.E.T withdrew at the very last moment due to the onerous conditions imposed by Crewe Corporation.

The Corporation applied for a similar scheme in 1900, and the B.E.T. again for 6¼ miles in 1901, with standard gauge tracks, but both schemes were rejected by the Light Railway Commissioners. A further Corporation scheme for 2½ miles was rejected by the ratepayers in 1902, and yet another which was dropped in 1904. Finally the Crewe and Nantwich Tramways Company was formed in February 1903, and proposed a four-mile tramway linking the two towns, but that is as far as it got, being dropped in October. The Railway Company provided many amenities for its workers, including schools, libraries, a mechanics institute and Queens Park. It also built a splendid electric power station, but alas, no electric tramway.

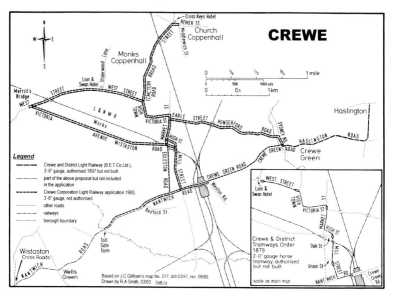

Northwich

A town of 18,000 by 1911, Northwich is situated on the River Weaver, 14 miles by rail to the north of Crewe. Its chemical industries were based on the salt, pumped up in the form of brine from the underlying rocks. The salt deposits were first exploited by the Romans, as indeed they still are to this day.

In 1901 the Warrington and Northwich Light Railway Company proposed lines from Northwich Station to Stockton Heath, at which point the route would branch to join end-on with the Latchford and Wilderspool routes of Warrington Corporation. However it was necessary to cross the Manchester Ship Canal at both points and the Ship Canal Company required an exorbitant annual sum to allow this to take place. Accordingly Warrington Corporation decided to apply for a Light Railway Order to cover the sections crossing the Ship Canal, being in a position to press the Canal Company not to make any charges, and in May 1903 Light Railway Orders were granted to the Warrington and Northwich Company and the Warrington Corporation, in the latter case as "the Stockton Heath Light Railways." In 1905 Warrington opened the quarter-mile extension from Wilderspool to Stockton Heath, after severe delays in equipping the swing bridge over the canal with safety devices. However no action was taken to build the 1¼ mile Latchford - Stockton Heath section and the powers for this lapsed.

The Square, Stockton Heath

One of the Brush built cars of 1920 stands at Stockton Heath terminus. The track to the right, leading off towards Stretton, was intended as a junction with the Warrington and Northwich Light Railway. *(Valentines card, courtesy Online Transport Archives*

The Warrington and Northwich Light Railway Order authorised an 11½ mile line from the Corporation's Stockton Heath terminus via Stretton and Marston into Northwich via Manchester Road, and through the town to Greenbank Station on the line to Chester. Also authorised was the alternative route, 7½ miles, back to Stretton via Winnington and Barnton. In 1906 the Company proposed to lay tracks from Stockton Heath to Stretton, some 2½ miles, providing Warrington would work this section, but the negotiations fell through when Warrington asked for a guarantee against any losses. No lines of this ambitious scheme, which would have provided a direct link between the two towns, were ever built, and the short length of line at Stockton Heath leading towards Northwich, was never used.

Other lines proposed by the same syndicate, Stockton Heath to Runcorn and Latchford to Knutsford, were stillborn, but the Runcorn-Widnes Transporter Bridge, with which they were also involved, was built and did open in 1905.

Warrington

The Borough of Warrington, sited on the River Mersey midway between Liverpool and Manchester, has a history going back to Saxon times, and prospered as a market town serving the Cheshire Plain to the south and the Lancashire towns to the north. The town has a variety of industries including wire, nails, soap and leather.

There were proposals for horse tramways in 1880, but these never went beyond the proposal stage and it was not until 21 April 1902 that the first electric tram ran to Latchford. The five-route system of 6.84 miles was complete by 29 November 1902 except for the Stockton Heath Light Railway, a ¼ mile extension from the Wilderspool terminus to Stockton Heath. This was opened on 7 July 1905 and crossed the Ship Canal on a swing bridge, protected by catch points on the southern side.

Authorised short extensions from the Cemetery terminus were never built, but the Warrington undertaking was a progressive one and trams and track were kept in good condition. The Latchford, Sankey Bridges and Cemetery routes were reconstructed during 1922, the latter with over half a mile of new double track. An Act obtained in 1920 permitted construction of a 10 chain linking line from Bridge Street to Buttermarket Street across the town centre which opened in 1922. The fleet, conventional single-truck double-deckers, initially open-top from Milnes, and in 1920 open-canopy cars from Brush, had also been vestibuled, top-covered and retrucked as required.

The Longford route had been built in the expectation that the South Lancashire Tramways Company would build the $4^1/_2$ mile line from Ashton-in-Makerfield via Newton-le-Willows, and so connect Warrington to the rest of the Lancashire system, but it was not to be and the Longford route was abandoned on 31 December 1931, three months after that to Stockton Heath. However it was not until 1935 that the remaining routes closed, the last tram, No.1, running to Latchford and back on 28th August.

Looking north through open country towards Newton-Le-Willows, to which a tramway was authorised, Warrington Corporation one-man car, No.18, waits at Longford terminus. *(National Tramway Museum.*

Atherton

Numerous small towns developed on the Lancashire Coalfield during the nineteenth century, with coalmining and textiles the main industries. Atherton, some 13 miles north east of Warrington, and a similar distance west of Manchester, by chance became the centre of the South Lancashire Tramways system.

A horse tramway to link Atherton with Leigh, a larger town and municipal borough three miles to the south, was proposed in the 1880's, and in 1896 a Leigh and District Tramways Company was proposed to build a 3ft. 6in. line from Lowton St. Mary's to Atherton Central (L&Y) Station, with two branches in Leigh. This failed to progress, but more ambitious schemes were afoot. First, was the Lancashire Light Railways Company Ltd. which proposed in 1898 to construct almost 24 miles of tramway, including a line linking St. Helens with Bolton via Leigh. This scheme was withdrawn in 1899, but soon revived by a new company, the South Lancashire Tramways Company.

South Lancashire No.3, after fitting of a top cover, is seen in Market Street, Leigh, on the Bolton service.

(National Tramway Museum

Under an Act of 1900, and a further Act in 1901, this company was authorised to build 75 miles, approximately one third double track, which, in addition, would have linked St. Helens with Bolton via Westhoughton, and Warrington with Bolton via Leigh and Hulton, Four Lane Ends. In the event the Hulton Lane - Four Lane Ends and Westhoughton - Deane sections were transferred to Bolton Corporation and opened in 1902 and 1924 respectively. The Act also granted powers to run over the Farnworth UDC tramways and to enter into running agreements with Warrington and Liverpool Corporations.

The Company now had its Act, but unfortunately not the capital to build the system. It therefore registered the South Lancashire Electric Traction and Power Company, which acquired the capital of the two earlier companies, to remedy the situation. To complete the company story the Lancashire United Tramways Ltd. was formed and took over on 1 January 1906.

Construction of the intended main line from St. Helens to Bolton eventually started in 1902, and on 20 October the section from the Leigh boundary at Lowton St. Mary's to Four Land Ends was opened. Work continued and completion of the line to St. Helens via Hindley and Ashton-in-Makerfield was celebrated on 30 March 1903 with a procession of six trams, three Liverpool and three South Lancashire, from Liverpool to Bolton, with a seventh, a Bolton car, joining the procession at Atherton. A through passenger service was never envisaged, although goods traffic to Liverpool using two-car units was seriously considered, but mainly due to lack of finance and the opposition of St. Helens, the scheme was never implemented. However a wide-ranging tram-based parcels service was introduced.

South Lancashire No.39, in original open-top condition, has arrived at Boothstown, probably on the opening day, 20 April 1905. *(Courtesy A.W.Brotchie.*

Extensions eastwards from Tyldesley, reached on 25 October 1902, were delayed for nearly three years; Boothstown, 2½ miles, was not opened until 20 April 1905; Swinton Church, a further four miles, and Walkden, three miles, opened on 27 September 1906, and the final link to Winton on 29 March 1907. It was now possible to run an electric tram through from Liverpool to beyond Manchester, and in fact a decorated Liverpool tram at least once travelled right through to Stockport and back.

Leigh Corporation had ambitions to be a tramway operator, and tended to make things difficult for the South Lancashire Company, with the result that the main SLT depot was built at Howe Bridge, in the Atherton district, rather than in Leigh as originally agreed and intended. Leigh did obtain an Act, the Leigh Corporation Act in 1903 for 3.64 miles of tramway, an east-west line from Plank Lane through the town along Manchester Road to Leigh Cemetery, this latter section duplicating the South Lancashire line to Boothstown within the Borough. However, nothing came of these proposals.

Through services were eventually introduced. Lowton St. Mary's to Bolton on 14 June 1909, withdrawn in 1915, but reinstated from Leigh to Bolton in 1927. St.Helens to Ashton started in October 1905, operated by the St.Helens Company, while the Winton to Worsley section was operated through from Manchester by Salford Corporation.

The South Lancashire Tramway system was now at its zenith with 37.17 miles of route, including 6.54 leased, operated by a variety of bogie and single-truck open-balcony tramcars housed in three depots, Atherton, Platt Bridge, and Swinton. The first abandonment, to trolleybuses, was the Atherton-Ashton route on 3 August 1930, and the last, operated by Company trams, Lowton St.Mary's-Leigh and Leigh-Bolton, on 16 December 1933, the latter replaced by a trolleybus service. The isolated Winton to Worsley section was replaced by Salford Corporation buses on 7 October 1936.

In contrast to the urban scenes in the two previous views, South Lancashire No.3 in open-top condition, is travelling towards Lowton through more open country. Trams never reached St. Helens by the direct route.

(National Tramway Museum

Farnworth

Although the tramways linking Bolton with Salford were discussed in our book *The Tramways of South-East Lancashire,* some reference is needed here. A double-track, standard-gauge horse tramway was opened between Bolton and Farnworth (Black Horse) on 3 June 1881, but the extension onwards to Clifton was not built at this time. The horse tram service ended on 1 January 1900 and was replaced by Bolton electric trams as far as Moses Gate the next day, but it was not until 13 April that they ran to the Black Horse.

Farnworth U.D.C. obtained an Act in 1900 authorising 5.65 miles of tramway, which the Council hoped would prove profitable in the tramway network which they envisaged would build up. In the same year Kearsley U.D.C. obtained a Provisional Order to construct $1^{3}/_{4}$ miles along the main Manchester Road to the boundary with Clifton.

Farnworth opened its line from Moses Gate to the boundary at Brookhouse on 9 January 1902 and can claim the distinction of being the first Urban District Council to operate an electric tramway. The Council also agreed to work the Kearsley line and this opened on 20 February 1902. Unfortunately the tramway was not a financial success and was leased to the South Lancashire Company from 1 April 1906. The Company built the Walkden Link and also leased the Kearsley line, which was worked to Clifton by Bolton Corporation from 14 june 1909 to 13 December 1915. Finally, on 1 February 1930, service 74, joint with Salford Corporation was introduced from the Black Horse to Manchester, but it lasted only until 28 February 1931. Following renewal of the Farnworth lease in 1927 Bolton Corporation had taken over operation of the services to the Black Horse and Walkden, using bogie and single-truck cars respectively. Due to the worn-out track these services were abandoned on 12 November 1944.

Wigan

Sited on the River Douglas, Wigan, the Roman Coccium, developed as a market town and was created a Borough in 1246. The building of the Leeds and Liverpool Canal in 1816, a link to the Bridgewater canal in 1820, a link to the Liverpool and Manchester Railway in 1832 and to the main line south in 1848, all promoted rapid industrial development based on local coal mines, iron foundries and cotton mills. Wigan was created a County Borough in 1889 and by the end of the century had, with Pemberton, a population of almost 85,000.

The first tramways in the town were authorised to the Wigan Tramways Company Ltd. under the Tramways Orders Confirmation Act of 1879. Unusually for Lancashire they were built to the narrow 3ft.6in. gauge, and the first line to Pemberton was opened with horse traction on 2 August 1880. The Hindley line followed in 1883, and steam traction with locally-built Wilkinson engines was introduced on 7 February 1882 to Pemberton and late in 1883 to Hindley. The last horse trams ran in April 1885. The Wigan Tramways Company was soon in financial difficulties and was succeeded in 1893 by the Wigan and District Tramways Company Ltd. The tracks were taken over by the Corporation and leased back to the Company , as was the line, newly built under the Act of 1893, to Platt Bridge. New Kitson locomotives were also introduced at this time.

By December 1899 the Corporation had decided to run its own tramways with electric traction still on the narrower 3ft.6in. gauge, and the first route, to Martland Mill, opened on 25 January 1901. It was followed by Wigan Lane on 7 June, and the steeply graded Scholes line on 20 December 1901, but it was not until 29 May 1903 that the Platt Bridge line was converted.

Meanwhile the Company had ambitions to run electric tramways in the district, and in 1899 it deposited plans for over seven miles of light railways outside the Borough, from Newtown to Platt Bridge via Bryn, Ashton-in-Makerfield and Bamfurlong, plus a branch along the Warrington Road through Abram. However the Corporation took over the profitable Company lines as from 1 October 1902 and reconstructed the steam lines, and the Platt Bridge line, to standard gauge in 1904-5. The last steam tram ran to Hindley on 26 September 1904, and the replacing electric trams finally reached Hindley on 4 October 1905 to connect with the South Lancashire service from Atherton to Haydock. This service covered the line from Ashton to Platt Bridge originally proposed by the Wigan Company in 1899.

Wigan Lane was also converted to standard gauge and extended to Standish on 5 July 1905. Here it would have linked with the proposed line to Coppull, Chorley and Preston authorised to the Preston, Chorley and Horwich Tramways Company in 1903. This was never built, nor did Wigan take up the offer to extend the Standish line the 2¼ miles to Coppull.

By April 1906, with extensions to Standish and Orrell (Abbey Lakes), in standard gauge, and Aspull in narrow gauge, the Wigan system was complete with 24½ miles of tramway, including 6½ miles narrow gauge and 5¼ miles leased, To operate the system there were 13 narrow-gauge open top, and 54 standard gauge single deck tramcars built at Preston and Motherwell.

The narrowness of some of the streets doubtless influenced the decision to adopt the narrow gauge for the initial routes, but by 1921 the tracks were worn out and a decision on their future had to be made. In the end the Aspull route was converted to standard gauge as far as the original terminus at New Springs in 1923, and the Martland Mill route was replaced by trolleybuses in 1926. At Hindley in 1927 the tracks were finally connected to the South Lancashire Market Street line, one third of a mile and disused for many years, and a through service, weekends only, to St.Helens via Ashton opened in April 1927.

Wigan Corporation No.41, a Hurst Nelson combination car, waits for passengers at Wigan Wallgate Station before the track was doubled in 1911-12.
This station on the Lancashire and Yorkshire Railway offered services to Manchester, Liverpool and Southport.

(Commercial card, courtesy A. W. Brotchie

These improvements were the last; the St.Helens service ended in May 1928 and the other routes succumbing, one by one, between 1928 and 28 March 1931. While the surplus narrow-gauge cars were either sold or scrapped, new double-deck balcony cars had been purchased, six in 1914 and a further six in 1920. These gave good service, and four of the earlier batch saw further use in South Shields.

St.Helens

St.Helens grew and prospered during the later part of the nineteenth century, its development based on the local coalfield and salt from nearby Cheshire. The building of the Sankey Brook Canal in 1757 and later railway links to Liverpool assisted its growth. To-day it is well known for the production of sheet glass. In 1868 the town was created a Borough, and ten years later William Busby of Liverpool put forward a tramway scheme. The St.Helens and District Tramways Co was incorporated in 1879, but construction was delayed and the first horse-drawn tram did not run until 5 November 1881, to Prescot. Further routes, to Peasley Cross, Denton's Green and Haydock brought the mileage up to 9.01 the following year.

The Company was not profitable and a new company, the St.Helens & District Tramways Co.Limited, was formed to introduce steam traction and took over on 1 October 1889. Steam traction using Green engines and Milnes double-deck bogie trailers replaced the horse trams on 4 April 1890 on all routes except Haydock which followed later.

The Corporation purchased the tramways under the Act of 1893, and leased them to the Company for 21 years from 1 October 1898. They had decided to electrify them, and in order to raise capital to purchase new cars the New St.Helens and District Tramways Co.Ltd. was formed, and took over the lease from 1 February 1899. Electric traction was inaugurated on the Denton's Green line some six months later, on 19 July 1899, and the last steam tram ran on 7 April 1900.

Meanwhile the tramways were being extended. In addition to the extension from Peasley Cross to St. Helens Junction, 200 yards short of the station on the original Liverpool and Manchester Railway, connections were in time made with the Liverpool system at Prescot and the South Lancashire system at Haydock. Services were introduced between St.Helens and the City boundary at Knotty Ash on 25 June 1902 and between St. Helens and Ashton-in-Makerfield in November 1909. A St. Helens-Liverpool service operated by St. Helens cars only lasted from 18 May 1903 to 13 December 1905, although through fares continued for some years.

The lease expired on 30 September 1919 and on the following day the Corporation became the operators of 18.94 miles of tramway and a fleet of 36 open-top single-truck tramcars, mainly built by Brush. As these had been insufficient to maintain the Company services, cars from the South Lancashire Company were also used. The seven cars used on the Liverpool and Prescot line which were housed in the St. Helens depot, were incorporated in the South Lancashire fleet.

St. Helens No.25 at the No.7 fare stage on the Prescot Road. This car, built by Brush in 1921, was until 1929 No.41 in the St.Helens' fleet. It survived until the closure of the system on 31 March 1936.

(C. S. Young, courtesy A. K. Kirby

The St. Helens Corporation took over the tramways with enthusiasm and renewed and improved much of the trackwork as well as purchasing eight new trams from Brush. A short-lived through service to Wigan (6 April 1927 to 27 May 1928) was introduced, as was an hourly service to Liverpool, but this lasted for only three months, from 13 December 1928 until 23 March 1929.

In the meantime, in 1927, part of the Rainhill service had been replaced by trolleybuses and this form of traction was introduced on the other routes during the next few years. The changeover was completed with the abandonment of the direct Prescot service on 31 March 1936.

Liverpool and St. Helens tramcars met at The Kings Arms, Prescot from 1 April 1921 until 31 March 1936. Liverpool Priestly car No.147 is entering the stub in Warrington Road while St. Helens Brush car No.25 of 1921 stands in St. Helens Road on 7 July 1935. Liverpool cars later terminated in St. Helens Road.

(A. M. Gunn)

Prescot

In medieval times Prescot was the more important town and by the mid-eighteenth century had been linked with Liverpool, St.Helens and Warrington by turnpike roads, but the nearest railway station was some half-mile to the south, hence a possible reason for tramway links to St.Helens and Liverpool.

However the first electric tramway at Prescot was in the grounds of the British Insulated Wire Company Ltd. on the Warrington Road, where the Simplex conduit system was demonstrated late in 1896. It was a side-slot line on which a single-deck tram was operated. The tram, built by Milnes, seated 20 passengers and had two 15hp GE 800 motors and GE K2 controllers. It was purchased by the South Lancashire Company in 1901 and advertised for private hire.

The Lancashire Light Railways Co. Ltd. was formed on 21 April 1898, the whole of the capital being owned by the Lancashire United Tramways Co.Ltd. Later in the year it obtained a Light Railway Order for a single-track line through open country from Brook Bridge, near Prescot, to the Liverpool City Boundary at Knotty Ash, 3.11 miles. This duly opened on 25 June 1902, but the link to Broad Green via Huyton, authorised to the South Lancashire Tramways Company, was never built. As already seen the line was the essential link in the chain of tramways from the cotton towns of Lancashire to the port of Liverpool. The promoters had hoped to introduce through goods services to the port, but although discussed for nearly twenty years they never materialised. The only through service was the short-lived passenger one from St.Helens to Liverpool.

Liverpool Corporation purchased the single-track and loop line, and from 1 October 1919 it became the outer part of a Liverpool-Knotty Ash-Brook Bridge service. This was an inconvenient terminus, and so in 1921 Liverpool purchased the half mile of track into Prescot centre. The tramway was rebuilt in 1921-22 as a reserved double-track line from Knotty Ash, and it gave excellent service, including a through service to St.Helens for a short time in 1928-29. The line was abandoned in stages, the Prescot to Long View Lane section on 26 June 1949, and from Page Moss on 4 March 1955.

Liverpool

The port of Liverpool dates back to the thirteenth century, and thanks to its position facing the Irish Sea it developed trade with Ireland and later North America, importing cotton, sugar and cereals. The Docks were served from 1893 to 1956 by the Liverpool Overhead Railway, using latterly 19 three-car electric trains on the $6^{1}/_{2}$ miles from Dingle in the south to Seaforth in the north, in adjacent Bootle.

The Pier Head was the focal point of the tramway system and no less than 37 all-day services terminated on the three loops laid in 1921 adjacent to the Mersey Ferry terminals. These loops were approached mostly by two main tramway arteries, Dale Street, mainly business orientated, and Lord Street, mainly shopping. In peak hours auxiliary an additional services terminated at Castle Street, Old Haymarket, and other city centre locations.

Nine trams are visible in this view of Liverpool Pier Head, the terminus for numerous services from the city's suburbs.

(Owen Owen Ltd. card, courtesy A. W. Brotchie

The earliest horse-drawn rail service was introduced on the Line of Docks Railway in March 1859. The vehicles had retractable flanged wheels which would leave the rails when railway wagons were encountered. It ran until the opening of the Overhead Railway in 1893. The first tramway was built from the Old Swan along the Prescot Turnpike road as far as the city boundary at Fairfield, but the proposed extension into the city centre was not authorised by the City Council. This line, owned by the later Liverpool Road and Railway Omnibus Company, opened on 2 July 1861, but closed within six months. The Liverpool Tramways Company had obtained the Liverpool Tramways Act in 1868, the first Act to authorise the conveyance of passengers on tramways in public streets, even before the 1870 general Act. It opened its first route, to Dingle, in 1869. The company was not particularly successful and in February 1876 it amalgamated with the Liverpool Road and Railway Omnibus Co., Ltd. to form the Liverpool United Tramways and Omnibus Company Ltd.

The track was taken over by Liverpool Corporation in 1880 and leased back to the company, which successfully built up a large network. By 1885 it comprised 17 routes, serving the city, 28.33 miles; West Derby, 5.29 miles; Walton-on-the-Hill, 3.25 miles; and Wavertree, 1.12 miles, these latter areas being absorbed into the city in 1895, and also the neighbouring Borough of Bootle-cum-Linacre, which opened in 1882 with 3.25 miles. This 41 mile network was served by over 250 double-deck tramcars built by Starbuck, Ashbury and at the Company's works, originally in Aigburth and from 1881 at Lambeth Road.

The Company experimented with mechanical traction during this period. The first steam trial took place on 28 November 1879 at Aigburth with an engine built for the Company by Duncan, Wilson. Although the trial was judged a success, nothing came of this or of the more extensive trials at Walton in November 1881 with the Duncan Wilson engine, another by R. & W Hawthorn of Newcastle, and a self propelled steam tramcar built to Apsey's patent by Omerod, Grierson and Company of Manchester. There was a demonstration of cable traction in the Company's yard at Kirkdale on 25 September 1883, and compressed air on the Bootle lines in 1884.

Liverpool Corporation No.111 stands at Aigburth Vale while a horse bus awaits passengers for Garston.

(National Tramway Museum

16

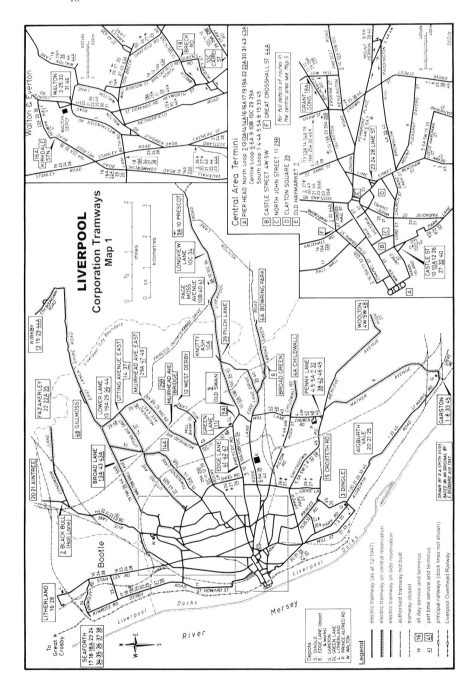

Liverpool Corporation No.68, for Old Haymarket, has just turned out of Strand Road into Stanley Road, Bootle, in 1910.

(W. H. S. Merseyside Series, Courtesy A. W. Brotchie.

The Company, including 21 car depots and stables, and the Lambeth Road Works, were taken over by the Corporation on 1 January 1897, but Company operation continued until the end of August. The Corporation immediately started the conversion to electric traction and the first electric trams, single-deck cars with trailers, ran to Dingle on 16 November 1898. Conversion of the remaining routes was rapidly carried out and the last horse tram ran in the city on 6 December 1902 and in Bootle, to Litherland, on 25 August 1903.

In the meantime the Garston and District Tramways Co., Ltd., owned by the South Lancashire Tramways group, had been constructing its tramway, authorised by an Act of 1900, from Aigburth to Garston. This was taken over in 1902 when Garston was absorbed into Liverpool. The 2 1 /2 mile single-track line, later rebuilt as double line, mainly on reserved track, opened on 28 August 1902. Liverpool pioneered the construction of reserved grass-track tramways, and the first such line was opened to Bowring Park in 1914, also nearly all the major extensions after that date were on side or centre reservation.

Liverpool Corporation continued to extend its tramway system over the next forty years; worthy of note was the purchase and reconstruction of the Prescot line already mentioned, the reserved track lines out to new housing estates in the 1930's, the linking of the Garston and Allerton termini on 4 July 1939 and finally, the long extension out to Kirkby, in the Rural District of Whiston, 10 miles from the Pier Head, was not completed until 12 April 1944. This well developed network of 97.6 miles, with 27.85 on reservation, was served by a fleet of 740 trams including some 360 modern bogie and single-truck cars built 1933-1942 in the Edge Lane workshops, opened 1928.

Although in 1945 the City Council was given the choice of a modern tramway system based mainly on reserved tracks, the bus option was chosen. The 10 year abandonment scheme got under way in 1948 with the withdrawal of the 26-27 Outer Circle service. This was followed by routes with portions of single or worn-out tracks, including some sections on reserved tracks. The closure of the Garston circle on 7 June 1953 saw the abandonment of the first high-quality reserved-track line. The remainder closed over the next four years concluding with services 6A and 40 to Bowring Park and Page Moss on 14 September 1957, by coincidence including the first reserved track, opened in 1914.

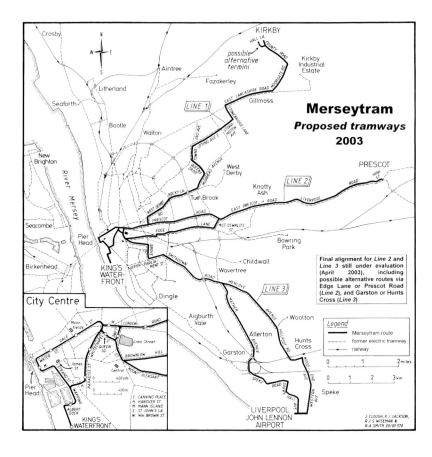

Merseytram

Plans for a three-line modern tramway system as part of an integrated transport network, are being progressed by Merseytravel and its partners. Line 1, expected to open in 2006-7, will link the city centre loop, serving the Pier Head, the Waterfront and railway stations, with Kirkby town centre. Line 2 will approximate to the original service 10 to Old Swan and Prescot. Line 3 will connect the city centre to Garston via Allerton, Hunts Cross and the John Lennon Airport at Speke.

Great Crosby

North of Liverpool and Bootle residential areas developed along the shores of the River Mersey. These were served by the Liverpool, Crosby and Southport Railway, later L.& Y.R., from 1850, and by horse buses from 1879. In the 1880's there were proposals to extend the horse trams from Seaforth, but no progress was made until 1897 when the Urban Districts of Waterloo-With-Seaforth and Great Crosby put forward plans for an electric tramway totalling 1.67 and 1.95 miles respectively. The Order was granted except for the branch to Blundellsands, of which 1.66 and 1.00 miles were built and operated.

At Seaforth Sands Station No.2 in the Great Crosby fleet waits for passengers from an incoming Overhead Railway train at the elaborate terminus of this 6½ mile dockside railway.

(Courtesy A. W. Brotchie.

The tramway, leased to the Liverpool Overhead Railway Company, was opened to Waterloo on 19 June 1900 and to Great Crosby on 1 September 1900. It was worked by a fleet of 14 uncanopied open-top cars built at nearby Preston together with two single-deck toastracks for summer use. By the time the line was abandoned 12 cars had been canopied of which nine had top-covers.

In 1918 the L.O.R. Company requested an extension of the lease to 1939, but instead the Councils entered into negotiations with Liverpool Corporation and in 1925 it was proposed that Liverpool should take over on 1 January 1926. It would widen the road, relay the line with double track, lower the road under a bridge, and extend its own Old Haymarket - Seaforth service to Great Crosby.

Unfortunately the proposed take over failed at the eleventh hour, and a service of 15 hired London General AEC B Type buses, provided by Waterloo & Crosby Motor Services Ltd., replaced the trams as from 1 January 1926, but were very soon replaced by new "NS" buses from London.

Southport

A residential seaside town with five miles of sandy beach facing the Irish Sea, Southport developed with the coming of the railways giving easy access to Liverpool and Manchester. The electrification of the Lancashire & Yorkshire line to Liverpool in 1904 gave a further impetus to this trend, and encouraged summer visitors to the town. Birkdale, an urban district to the south, was amalgamated with Southport in 1912.

Horse tramways were introduced by the Southport Tramways Company Ltd. on 31 May 1873, with a standard-gauge line from Churchtown through the town to Birkdale Station using open-top four-wheelers. Another company, the Birkdale and Southport Tramways Company, introduced horse trams on 12 May 1883 from Kew Gardens to London Square, both in Southport, later extended to the Crown Hotel in Birkdale.

A busy scene in Lord Street, Southport. No. 36 for Cambridge Road passes No. 37 on route 2 to the Crown Hotel in the late 1920's. These trams were built open top by Brush for the Southport Company in 1901. They were top covered from 1920 onwards,

(F.B.Walton, courtesy A.K.Kirby.

Both Southport Corporation and Birkdale U.D.C purchased the tramways in their respective areas in 1900, the Corporation electrifying and extending the Birkdale Company lines, while the Southport Company, now within the British Electric Traction group, continued to work their lines, electrified them, and operated them on a 21 year lease until 28 February 1918, although the lease expired on 31 January.

Southport Corporation opened its electric tramways on 18 July 1900, and the Company did likewise on 11 August a year later. It completed its system with an extension to Smedley's Hydro in August 1903. The Corporation had a fleet of open-top double-deck and single-deck 'California' cars plus a toastrack car. The Company had a fleet of well-appointed double-deck cars from Brush, and one of the first regenerative demi-cars.

Two interurban tramways were authorised from Southport in 1900. These were an Ormskirk and Southport Light Railway, 6½ miles, standard gauge, and a line across the Ribble Estuary to Lytham described in *The Tramways of North Lancashire*. Neither line was built.

Following the unification of the two systems on 1 January 1918 there was a short extension in the summer of 1924 of the Cemetery route beyond the Borough boundary to Crescent Road, together with a branch to Bedford Park to serve new housing. This, however, was the last, and contraction of the system started in March 1931 and was completed on 31 December 1934.

This is hardly surprising as the average speed was only 7mph and although the trams had been top covered the electrical equipment was outdated. However the trams did well during the summer holiday season. Their most successful enterprise was the 'Grand Tour' introduced in April 1914 and operated by toastrack trams. It ran from London Square to Kew Gardens and back to the centre via St. Lukes Road.

Southport Pier

The wide gently-sloping sandy beach at Southport with a great tidal range, was ideal for pier construction. It was built in 1860, the first to be built of iron in the country. At 1465 yards it was the second longest after Southend.

A tramway with a carriage pushed by hand was introduced by the Pier Company in 1863. The pier was widened in 1865, and a new cable-worked 3ft.6in. gauge line was laid on the south side and opened on 5 March 1866. The line was converted to electric working using third-rail current collection in 1905. It was worked by a three-car train, a closed motor car with open trailers fore and aft. The 1079 yard line was taken over by the Corporation in 1936 and the bodies were replaced by new ones based on the Blackpool railcoaches. The tramway in its turn was scrapped in 1950 and replaced by a 1ft. 11½ in. (600cm) gauge miniature railway. This opened on 27 May 1950 and was worked by diesel power until closed in 1998.

Cars from two different companies at the Woodside terminus, Birkenhead. Milnes car No.12 of the Birkenhead United Company is on the Prenton Service. Note this car has no decency boards. The car behind is a Wirral Company car on the New Ferry service. Behind the trams the wheels of cabs can be seen, where they stand for hire. Woodside Ferry is the terminus of the present Museum line.

(Martin Jenkins collection.

Birkenhead

Linked to Liverpool by ferry, and later by the Mersey Railway opened in 1886 and electrified in 1903, Birkenhead developed rapidly after the first dock was opened in 1847. The docks and associated industries, including shipbuilding, continued to expand until 1933 when the dock at Bidston was opened.

The town's claim to fame is its street tramway, the first purpose-built line in the British Isles to carry passengers. The Birkenhead Street Railway Company Ltd. was promoted by George F. Train and opened from Woodside Ferry to Birkenhead Park with due ceremony on 30 August 1860. In 1861 it was extended to Oxton, and in 1864 it was rebuilt by the Birkenhead Town Commissioners and leased back to the Company, the original step rails, laid to a gauge of 5ft.2in. or 5ft.2½in., being replaced by grooved rail to standard 4ft.8½in. gauge. The Company which had no statutory powers, was reconstituted as the Birkenhead Tramways Company in 1877 and continued to serve the town until 1890.

It is interesting to note that by 1881 with a population of 84,000 the town supported three separate horse tramway companies. the Birkenhead Tramways Company; the Hoylake & Birkenhead Rail & Tramway Company with a line along the docks opened on 6 September 1873, and the Wirral Tramway Company Ltd. The latter's line to New Ferry opened on 28 March 1877. When complete these three lines totalled 10.82 miles worked by a fleet of 37 cars, built locally at the Cleveland Street works of George Starbuck, which were taken over by George F. Milnes in 1886.

Further amalgamations followed. The Hoylake Company's tramway was purchased by the B.T.C. in 1879, which in turn was bought out by Birkenhead Corporation, who leased the lines back to a new Birkenhead United Tramways Omnibus and Carriage Company Ltd., which continued operation from 1890 until 1901. The Wirral Company's line meanwhile was purchased by the Corporation in 1895 and leased back for 21 years. However it was bought outright by agreement late in 1899, and electric trams introduced on this always isolated line, on 4 February 1901.

The United Company's lines were purchased in 1900, electrified the following year and extended to Higher Tranmere, Claughton, and Oxton via Balls Road to complete the system of 13.55 miles in 1902. In 1909 a short extension in Market Place South brought the mileage up to 13.70.

Two features are worth recording; the low bridge at Chester Street on the New Ferry route required single-deck cars until lowbridge double-deck bogie cars were purchased from Hurst Nelson in 1913, and the impressive six-track layout at Woodside Terminus. In the latter days of the system in 1937, a wide variety of single-truck and bogie tramcars could be seen here awaiting passengers emerging off the ferries.

Tramway abandonment began with the isolated New Ferry service in December 1931 and concluded with the Oxton and Claughton circular on 17 July 1937.

Wallasey

The north-east corner of the Wirral Peninsula developed as a residential area for Liverpool, to which it was connected by three ferries. Thus the small village of Wallasey expanded and merged with the nearby settlements of Seacombe, Egremont, Liscard, Poulton and New Brighton, the latter becoming a popular seaside resort.

The Wallasey Tramways Order of 1871 authorised four miles of tramway to the Wallasey Tramways Co.Ltd., but the capital could not be raised and the company was dissolved in 1874. The new Wallasey Tramways Company was more successful and obtained the Wallasey Tramways Act of 1878. This authorised two standard-gauge lines from Seacombe to New Brighton, but only the inland route, 3.26 miles, via Rake Lane was built. It opened on 30 June 1879, and was operated successfully, from 1891 by the Wallasey United Tramway and Omnibus Company Ltd. with seven double-deck horse cars until 1 April 1901.

The Council then took over until it re-opened with electric traction on 17 March 1902. The direct Seabank Road route followed three days later. Further routes were opened in 1910-11 to bring the mileage up to 12.01, with two-thirds of this being double track. Unfortunately the cost of track renewal was too high, and the profitable trams were abandoned during 1929 to 1933, the last car running on the last day of November.

The fleet of 77 double-deck, single-truck cars was delivered in batches of 5 to 20 over the years 1902-1920, initially open-top, soon fitted with Magrini covers; later with covers, but unroofed balconies. In inclement weather flags were flown from the trolley ropes to indicate that the New Brighton and Egremont ferries were not running.

Birkenhead Corporation No. 12 built by Milnes in 1901 awaits departure from New Ferry terminus. The Birkenhead and Chester tramways Co.Ltd. had in 1902 proposed extending this tramway through to Chester, some fourteen miles to the south.

(Courtesy A.W. Brotchie.

The unique feature of the Wallasey trams was that all four basic services ran from Seacombe to New Brighton, connecting at both ends with Council-owned ferries to Liverpool. Four trams, up to ten at peak hours, would leave at ten-minute intervals. Dummy clocks on the car platform showed the time of the departing ferry with which the tram connected.

In 1900 the North Wirral Electric Tramway Company was proposing to build an electric tramway linking Wallasey and Birkenhead via Hoylake, West Kirby, Frankby and Upton, but the local authorities and the Wirral Railway were opposed. However, the Birkenhead and Chester Tramways Co., Ltd., registered in 1902, made more progress, and 15 miles of electric interurban tramway from New Ferry to Chester, with a branch to Eastham Ferry, was included in the Birkenhead and Chester Tramway Bill of 1903. Due to opposition from the railway companies the Bill was withdrawn and the company wound up in 1905.

Chester

The city of Chester, Castra Devana, was founded by the Romans, and is sited on the right bank of the River Dee. The city walls, nearly two miles in circumference, were rebuilt in AD 907 and are still intact today. The city declined as a port due to the silting of the Dee, but this attractive place still has a variety of industries, including tourism.

The Chester Tramways Company was formed in 1878, and the standard-gauge line, a little over two miles in length, was opened from the General Station to the Castle on 10 June 1879. It was extended to Saltney close to the Welsh border five weeks later. An eventual total of eleven double-deck cars from various makers were acquired, and one car, No.9, was used experimentally with a motor driven by compressed air. Four or five cars, more on race days, provided a regular service, which continued under Corporation ownership from 1 January 1902 until the end of the year.

CHESTER SCENES

Two Milnes tramcars stand side-by-side in the architectural splendour of Eastgate Street in Chester.

(National Tramway Museum

Looking across the border into Wales, No.2 in the Chester fleet is admired by the onlookers at Saltney terminus.

(National Tramway Museum

Regent Street and Infirmary Wrexham

One of the ten open-top Brush Cars, possibly No.6, of the Wrexham Company heads westwards along Regent Street.

(Valentines card, courtesy A.W.Brotchie

Electrification and rebuilding of the track to the narrower 3ft. 6in. gauge followed acquisition, and electric services began over the same route on 6 April 1903. An extension eastwards to Boughton in 1906 brought the mileage up to 3.59. A further half-mile extension along the Tarvin Road to Vicars Cross was authorised early in 1914 to Chester Rural District Council, but due to the outbreak of war it was not built.

Seventeen double-deck, uncanopied cars built by Milnes and U.E.C., together with a Brush demi-car which saw little use, maintained services for 27 years, the last tram running in the late afternoon of 15 February 1930. Used by the replacing municipal buses, the 1878 depot is still in use in 2003.

Wrexham

Twelve miles to the south of Chester, well west of the Dee valley and just within Wales, Wrexham developed as a market town and later in the nineteenth century industries developed based on nearby coalmines. The Wrexham District Tramways Company was formed in 1874 and soon obtained powers to build a 3ft. gauge tramway from the town southwards along the main road to Ruabon, some five miles to the south. A one-car service between Wrexham and Johnstown began in October 1876 and continued until April 1901, latterly with three double-deck tramcars, two from Starbuck, and one locally made.

The Wrexham and District Electric Tramways.Ltd. was registered by the B.E.T. in 1901 and during the next two years this company rebuilt the line, and extended it along the Mold road to the racecourse and, at the Johnstown end, to Duke Street a little short of the authorised terminus in Rhos village. Electric service with ten conventional double-deck cars from Brush began on 4 April 1903. The authorised 1½ mile extension to Ruabon was never built.

Although there were minor track improvements in the town centre, by 1925 the tracks were worn and the cars dilapidated, so services ceased at the early date of 31 March 1927 when No.9 returned to the depot just after midnight.

Rhyl

Chester's electric trams terminated at Saltney, 100 yards short of the Welsh border. Proceeding north-west along the estuary, a tramway was proposed in 1903 from Connah's Quay via Flint to Holywell, and back via Mold to Connah's Quay, but it was not progressed further.

Thirty miles west along the coast from Chester or fourteen from Holywell, we arrive at the seaside resort of Rhyl. Here, in 1883, a 3ft. 6in. gauge tramway was authorised to link Rhyl with Rhuddlan, 2.2 miles inland, but it was never built. In 1897 the Llandudno Company intended to extend its proposed Llandudno-Colwyn Bay line a further twelve miles to Rhyl and on to Prestatyn. These proposals were later taken over by the Rhyl and Prestatyn Light Railway Company, who obtained powers for them in 1900 but allowed them to lapse.

In 1952, Mr. Claude Lane of Modern Electric Tramways built a single-track, 15-inch gauge miniature tramway at Rhyl, a quarter mile long, round three sides of Voryd Amusement Park. The equipment came from St.Leonards, Hastings, where it had operated during the 1951 season. Owing to local opposition here the contract was not renewed, so he moved the tramway to Voryd Park. Here it operated seasonally, Whitsun to September, from 1952 until 1957. Four tramcars taking power at 60 volts DC were used. They were No.23, based on Darwen, later Llandudno 23, Blackpool "boat" No 225, an open-top car No.3, and an open toastrack No.6. These seated 20 small children, 12, 20 and 24 adults respectively.

Mr. Lane ran the tramway for the 1952 and 1953 seasons, but then transferred to Eastbourne where he built a 2 ft. gauge line, which opened on 4 July 1954, and finally to Seaton where the 2ft.9in. gauge tramway opened in 1970. This still operates and is fully described in our book *The Tramways of South West England*. However the Rhyl Tramway was very popular and continued to be operated on lease by the owners of the park until the end of the 1957 season.

Llandudno

The building of the railway to Holyhead and the splendour of the North Wales coastline soon attracted holiday makers to the area, and resorts developed rapidly to serve them. Llandudno was linked by a branch line in 1858, but there was no direct line from here to Rhos or Colwyn Bay, five miles to the east. There was thus scope for a tramway, and a number of schemes were put forward from 1892 onwards, which did not progress further.

The first powers were granted to the Llandudno and Colwyn Bay Light Railway Company under the Llandudno and Colwyn Bay Light Railway Order confirmed on 2 June 1899. This included the extension to Prestatyn aforementioned. Although a contract was let early in 1904 for the construction of the line to Rhos, where the depot was to be built, no work was done. A new company, the Llandudno and Colwyn Bay Electric Traction Co., Ltd., took over in 1906, and started work, but failed to raise the necessary finance and went into liquidation. Finally the Llandudno and District Electric Tramway Construction Co. Ltd. was registered on 25 July 1906, and in conjunction with Bruce Peebles & Co. Ltd. work got under way in 1907, and the 3ft. 6in. gauge line, from West Shore, Llandudno, to Rhos Depot, was opened on 19 October 1907. It was extended in stages; to Colwyn Bay on 7 June 1908 and on to Old Colwyn on 26 March 1915, a total of 8.37 miles. However the authorised extension at the Llandudno end, to Deganwy Station, was not built apart from the first 370 yards along West Parade, which was abandoned in 1917.

Llandudno No.17(ii), ex-No.14, on a special working, leaves Rhos Promenade for Colwyn Bay on 25 September 1955.

(R.J.S.Wiseman

The Company, which changed its name in 1909 to the less cumbersome Llandudno and Colwyn Bay Electric Railway Ltd., had doubled most of the original single track between 1912 and 1928. The original rolling stock, 22 single-deck cars, including 4 open toastracks, was augmented or replaced by second hand purchases from Accrington and Bournemouth. In 1946 two modern double-deck bogie cars from Darwen were purchased, but sadly these saw little use, being restricted to local services at each end of the line.

The Llandudno tramway offered a wide range of vistas, sea views, street scenes, cross-country runs through Bodafon Fields, the climb over the Little Orme, the eroding coastline along the toll road beyond, the Promenade and right-angled bend at Rhos and finally the cruise down the busy Conway Road to the terminus. It was a sad day indeed when the line was closed on Saturday 24 March 1956. If it had survived a few more years the serious efforts which were made to save at least part of it would have succeeded.

Great Orme Tramway

This line, also at Llandudno, was originally owned by the Great Orme Tramways Company and opened in 1902-03. It was built in two sections to the 3ft. 6in. gauge, with a halfway station which has been recently rebuilt. The line climbs 600 feet in little more than a mile with a maximum gradient of 1 in 3.6 on the lower section. Cable traction is employed, and the cable and pulleys are carried in a central conduit on the lower paved section, and above the ground on sleepers on the physically- separated upper section. The winding gear situated in the halfway station was steam driven until replaced by electricity in the winter of 1957-58.

The line was saved when taken over by Llandudno Urban District Council on 1 January 1949. It is now owned by Deganwy District Council and still operates during the summer season, with the four long bogie saloon cars built by Hurst Nelson in 1902.

No.4 of the Great Orme Tramway is seen on the lower section on 7 June 1954.

(R.J.S.Wiseman

Pwllheli

Continuing along the coast for some 40 miles via Bangor and Caernarfon and across the Lleyn Peninsula, we reach the port of Pwllheli. With fine beaches the town developed as a seaside resort during the last decades of the eighteenth century. To serve the beach the Corporation opened a short half-mile, believed 2ft.6in. gauge, horse tramway on 24 July 1899. It was worked during the summer only, by three single-deck cars built by the Midland Carriage & Waggon Company of Shrewsbury. It was never electrified and closed in the summer of 1920.

Earlier in 1894 a mineral tramway had been built to convey stone from a quarry to build the Promenade. This was converted into a passenger horse tramway during the summer of 1897,and later extended to run from Pwllheli Station to Llanbedrog, 3.88 miles to the west along the shore of Tremadoc Bay. It was worked by a variety of single-deck trams, including, from 1920, the three Corporation vehicles.

Built for much of its length on the sand dunes most of it was washed away by high seas during a fierce gale on the night of 28 October 1927, and early in 1928 it was decided not to rebuild it.

The Cambrian railway reached Pwllheli in 1867, but proposals to build a railway across the Peninsula to Porth Dinllaen came to naught, as did an electric tramway proposed, first in 1900 and later in 1903. The latter was for a Light Railway Order by the North Wales & District Light Railway & Electric Power Syndicate Ltd. for the Pwllheli, Nevin & Porth Dinlleyn Light Railway. This standard gauge line, 10½ miles to Porth Dinllaen plus the Nefyn branch, 1.65 miles, was authorised but never built, and the Cambrian Railway introduced a bus service in June 1906 in its place.

Llanbedrog Tramway. One of the open trams is standing at the Pwllheli town terminus. It is ready to take a good load of passengers for a four-mile trip along the seashore.

(Photochrom card, courtesy National Tramway Museum

Minor Lines

At Harlech a short tramway, three quarters of a mile long, and believed to be of 2ft. gauge, was built from the Cambrian Railway, a quarter mile south of its station, to the beach. It was worked by horses and opened in July 1878, but was closed in 1883 or soon afterwards.

At Fairbourne, near Barmouth, a 2ft gauge horse tramway ran north to Penrhyn Point Ferry. In 1911 it changed hands and in 1916 the gauge was narrowed and it was thereafter worked as a miniature railway with steam locomotives, in which form it still exists. At Aberystwyth, well to the south in mid-Wales, a funicular cliff lift still operates up Constitution Hill.

To the east, on the far side of the Welsh Mountains ,is Chirk where the Glyn Valley Tramway ran a roadside steam tramway for 7 $\frac{1}{2}$ miles to Glynceiriog and Hendre on the unusual 2ft. 4 $\frac{1}{2}$ in gauge. It was worked as a horse tramway from 1873 to 1888 with four cars, and then as a steam tramway until 1933, using 14 four-wheeled coaches and three locomotives with enclosed motion. Freight traffic continued until 1935.

The numerous narrow-gauge steam railways, 'The Great Little Trains of Wales' are well promoted and do not come within the scope of this book, but it is worth mentioning that the Corris Railway, a purely steam line, was for 33 years of its long life a member of the Imperial Tramways Group and managed by the Bristol Tramways and Carriage Company Ltd.

Warrington Corporation No.25, built by Brush in 1919, standing in Latchford village on 17 April 1935, four months before closure.

(C. S. Young courtesy A. K. Kirby

SOUTH LANCASHIRE CONTRASTS

South Lancashire Tramways No.17 in original condition at Pennington in 1902.

(T. Boothroyd, National Tramway Museum

South Lancashire Tramways No.82 with English Electric top-cover is at Walkden, turning from Manchester Road, (A6), into Bolton Road.

(Courtesy Alan Ralphs

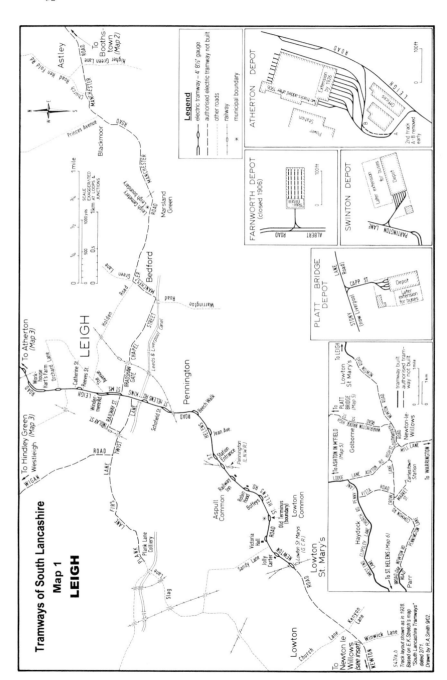

Tramways of South Lancashire
Map 1
LEIGH

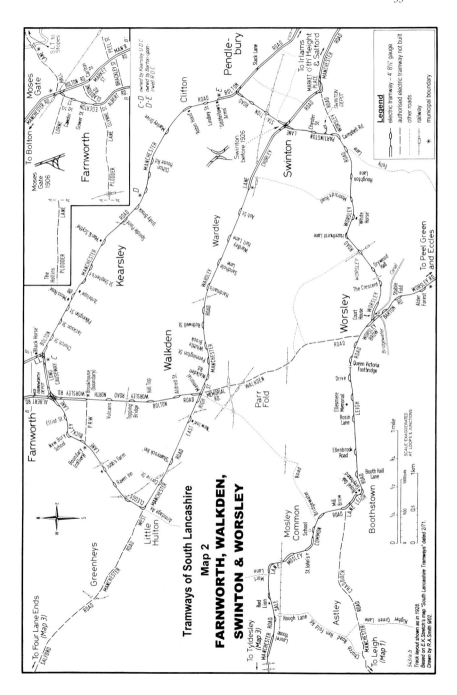

Tramways of South Lancashire
Map 2
FARNWORTH, WALKDEN,
SWINTON & WORSLEY

Legend

electric tramway – 4' 8½" gauge
authorised electric tramway not built
other roads
railway
municipal boundary

543/a.b
Track layout shown as in 1928.
Based on E.K.Stretch's map "South Lancashire Tramways" dated 2/71.
Drawn by R.A.Smith 9/02.

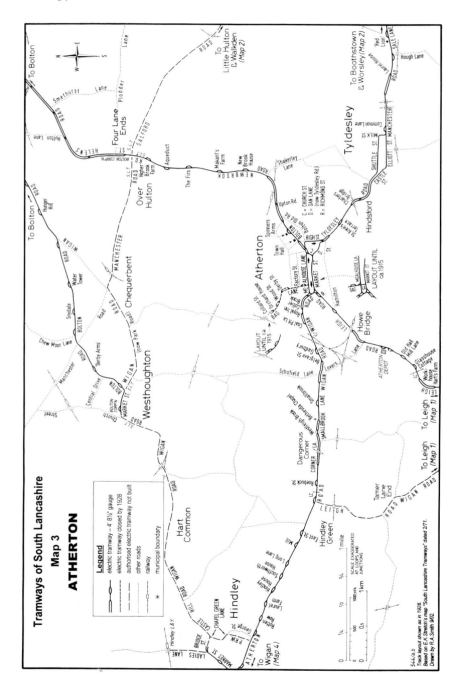

Tramways of South Lancashire

Map 3

ATHERTON

Legend

electric tramway – 4 8½ gauge
electric tramway closed by 1928
authorised electric tramway not built
other roads
railway
municipal boundary

544/2.b
Track layout shown as in 1928.
Based on E.K.Stretch's map 'South Lancashire Tramways' dated 2/71.
Drawn by R.A.Smith 9/02.

WIGAN CONTRASTS - 1

Wigan & District Wilkinson engine No.3 with an Eades reversible trailer fitted with a light roof on the upper deck.

(Dr. H. A. Whitcombe, Science Museum, Science and Society Picture Library

A Kitson engine with bogie trailer at Pemberton terminus.

(Dr. H. A. Whitcombe, Science Museum, Science and Society Picture Library

Corporation Tramways No.1 outside Martland Mill.

(Courtesy R. Brook

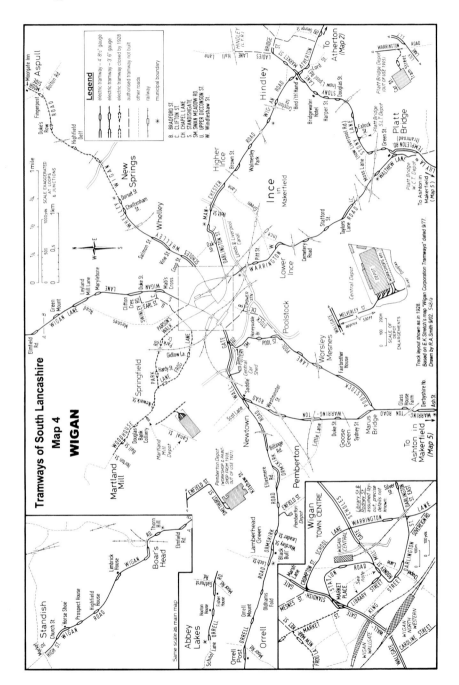

Tramways of South Lancashire
Map 4
WIGAN

WIGAN CONTRASTS - 2

No.40, a shortened Hurst Nelson car of 1904, at Ashton on the connecting curve to the South Lancashire system, photographed about 1927.

(Dr. H. A. Whitcombe, Science Museum, Science and Society Picture Library

No.90, one of twelve trams built by the local firm of Massey Brothers, at Abbey Lakes terminus on the last day of operation, 28 March 1931.

(Tramway Museum Society

38

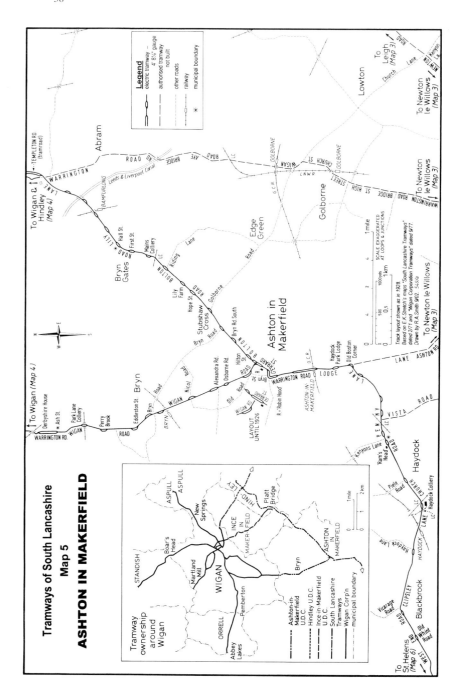

Tramways of South Lancashire

Map 5

ASHTON IN MAKERFIELD

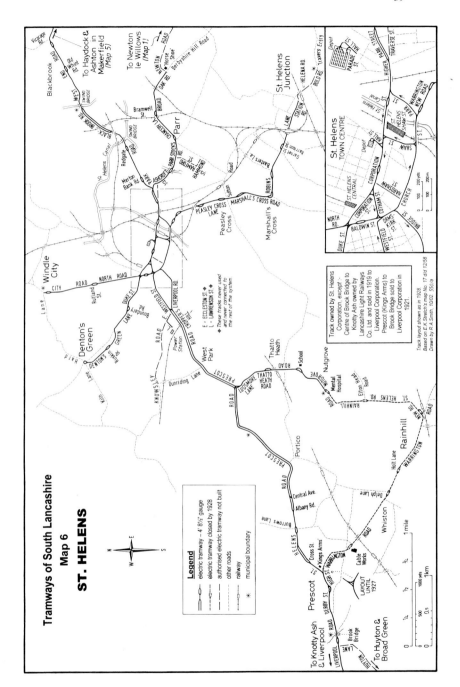

Tramways of South Lancashire

Map 6

ST. HELENS

39

Legend

electric tramway - 4' 8½" gauge
electric tramway closed by 1928
authorised electric tramway not built
other roads
railway
municipal boundary

Track owned by St. Helens
Corporation, except :-
Centre of Brook Bridge to
Knotty Ash owned by
Lancashire Light Railways
Co. Ltd and sold in 1919 to
Liverpool Corporation.
Prescot (Kings Arms) to
Brook Bridge sold to
Liverpool Corporation in
1921

Track layout shown as in 1928
Based on E.K. Stretch's map No. 17 d/d 12/58
Drawn by R A Smith. 10/02. 550/a

E = ECCLESTON ST. ✦
L = LAWRENSON ST. ✦
✦ These tracks never used
and never connected to
the rest of the system

St. Helens
TOWN CENTRE

St. Helens
Junction

To Haydock &
Ashton in
Makerfield
(Map 5)

To Newton
le Willows
(Map 1)

Blackbrook

Parr

Peasley
Cross

Marshall's
Cross

Windle
City

Denton's
Green

West
Park

Thatto
Heath

Nutgrove

Rainhill

Prescot

To Knotty Ash
& Liverpool

To Huyton &
Broad Green

ST. HELENS CONTRASTS

St. Helens & District Eades car No.1 in Ormskirk Street, with trace horse attached for the hills on the route to Prescot.

(Courtesy A. W. Brotchie

New St. Helens open-top bogie car No.4 on Green Lane en-route to Denton's Green.

(Commercial card, courtesy A. W. Brotchie

41

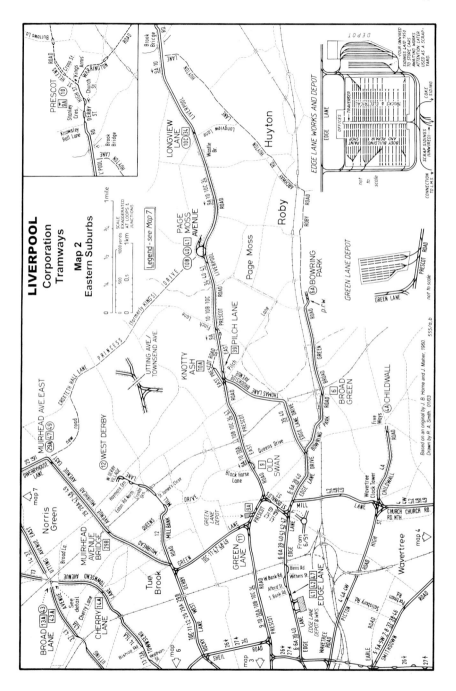

42

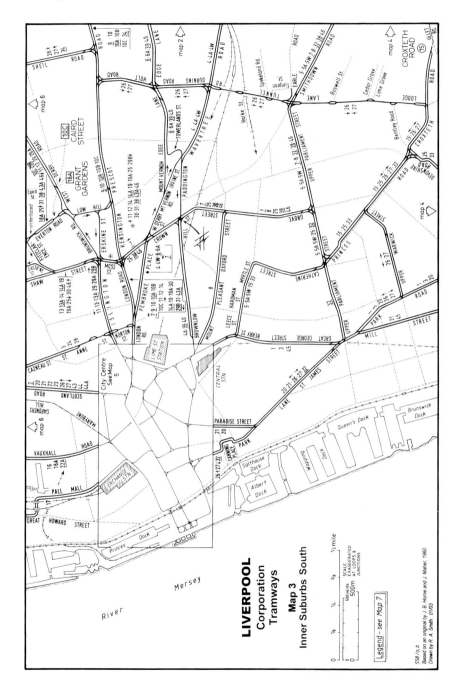

LIVERPOOL
Corporation
Tramways
Map 3
Inner Suburbs South

Legend – see Map 7

558/a,b
Based on an original by J. B. Horne and J. Maher, 1960.
Drawn by R. A. Smith, 01/03

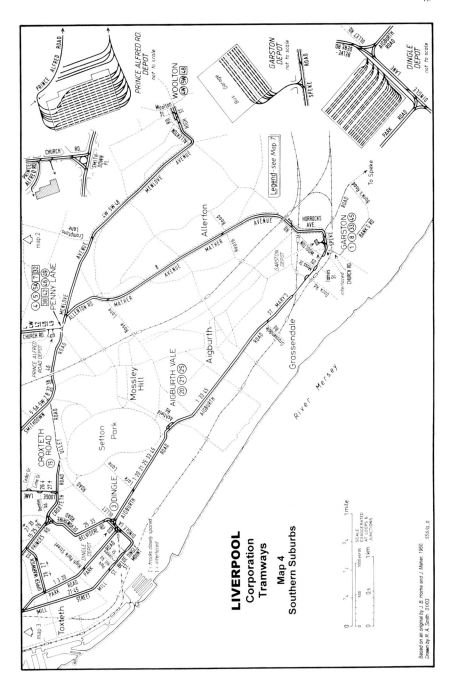

LIVERPOOL
Corporation
Tramways

Map 4
Southern Suburbs

Based on an original by J. B. Horne and J. Maher, 1960.
Drawn by R. A. Smith. 01/03

556/a, b

44

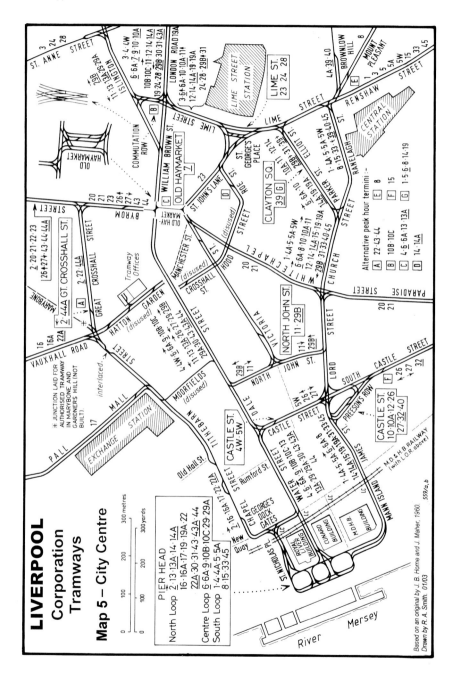

LIVERPOOL
Corporation Tramways

Map 5 – City Centre

Based on an original by J. B. Horne and J. Maher, 1960.
Drawn by R. A. Smith. 01/03

559/a, b

PIER HEAD
North Loop 2·13·13A·14·14A
16·16A·17·19·19A·22
22A 30·31·43·43A 44
Centre Loop 6·6A 9·10B·10C 29·29A
South Loop 1·4·4A·5·5A
8·15·33·45

Alternative peak hour termini:-
A 22·43·44
B 10B·10C
C 4·6·6A·13·13A
D 14·14A

E 8
F 15
G 1·5·6·8·14·19

THE EVOLVING LIVERPOOL TRAM - 1

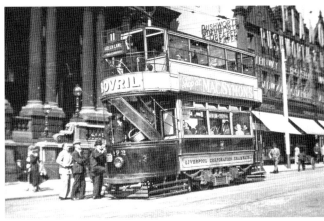

Preston Car No.172, fitted with Bellamy roof, loads passengers in Islington for Green Lane via West Derby Road.

(National Tramway Museum

Priestly Balcony Car No.363 at Seaforth terminus. Built open-top in 1902 it was top covered by 1905.

(H. B. Priestley, National Tramway Museum

English Electric car No.762, now preserved in Birkenhead, on a service 10B extra to Lime Street, Commutation Row photographed on 8 June 1953 in Prescot Road.

(R. J. S. Wiseman

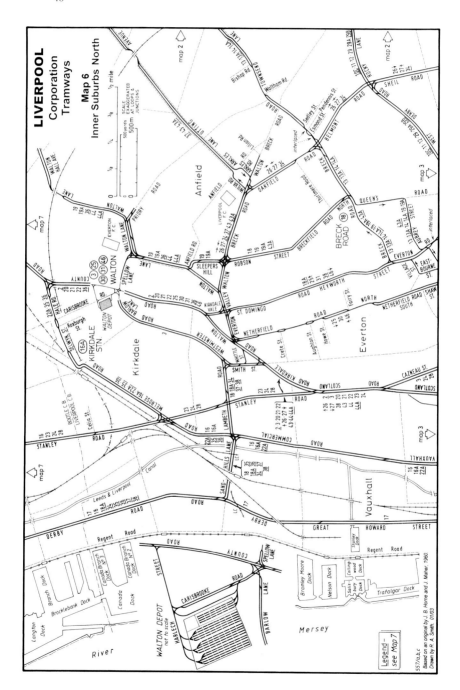

LIVERPOOL
Corporation
Tramways

Map 6
Inner Suburbs North

THE EVOLVING LIVERPOOL TRAM - 2

Domed roof car No.811 leaves Walton depot for service on 8 June 1953.

(R.J.S.Wiseman

Liverpool was a city with numerous complicated junctions. On 3 April 1954 No.978 is seen crossing the fossilised junctions at Sleepers Hill.

(R.J.S.Wiseman

'Baby Grand' No.222 on a 10B working at Low Hill junction on the same day.

(R.J.S.Wiseman

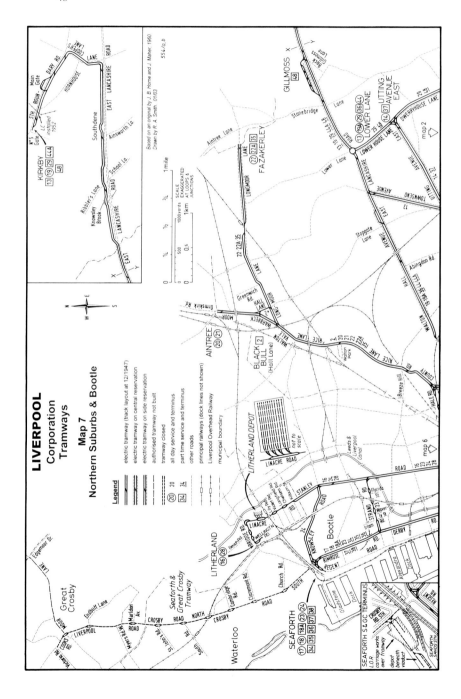

LIVERPOOL
Corporation
Tramways

Map 7
Northern Suburbs & Bootle

Legend

electric tramway (track layout at 12/1947)
electric tramway on central reservation
electric tramway on side reservation
authorised tramway not built
tramway closed
all day service and terminus
part time service and terminus
other roads
principal railways (dock lines not shown)
Liverpool Overhead Railway
municipal boundary

Based on an original by J. B. Horne and J. Maher, 1960
Drawn by R. A. Smith 01/03

SCALE
EXAGGERATED
AT LOOPS &
JUNCTIONS

KIRKBY

GILLMOSS

UTTING AVENUE EAST

LOWER LANE

FAZAKERLEY

AINTREE

BLACK BULL
(Hall Lane)

LITHERLAND DEPOT

LINACRE ROAD

LITHERLAND

Bootle

Great Crosby

Waterloo

Seaforth & Great Crosby Tramway

SEAFORTH

SEAFORTH S & GC TERMINUS

CONTRASTS AT WATERLOO

Left:- Canopied car No.12 at the Five Lamps, and right single-deck 'toastrack car No.10 on Crosby Road passes St.John's Road.

(Commercial cards courtesy A.W.Brotchie

In the 1930's Liverpool opened miles of new tracks to serve the developing suburbs to the north. Here No.880 is seen on Utting Avenue East, opened on 12 June 1937.

(R.J.S.Wiseman

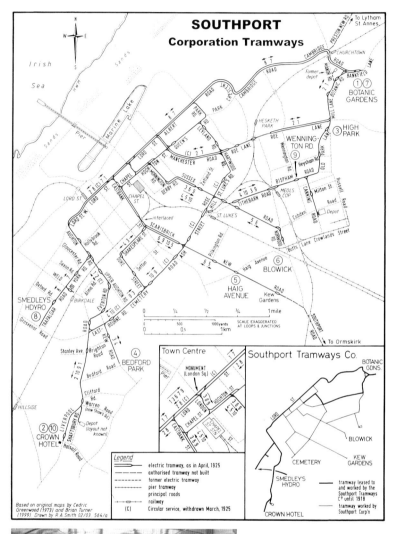

SOUTHPORT

Corporation Tramways

Liverpool Luxury Travel. Upper Saloon of No.280.

(J.C. Gillham

SOUTHPORT AND WALLASEY

Southport Corporation No.12 on the Chapel Street one-way terminal loop on service K, Kew Gardens, serving the zoo.

(Valentine's XL Series, courtesy A.W.Brotchie

Looking north along Liscard Road, Wallasey Corporation No.22 bound for New Brighton via Rake Lane passes Central Park.

(Moorhouse card, courtesy of A.W.Brotchie

Wallasey No.52 was later fitted with a Bellamy roof and is seen on Broadway on the Prenton route in 1933.

(H.Hughes, courtesy Martin Jenkins.

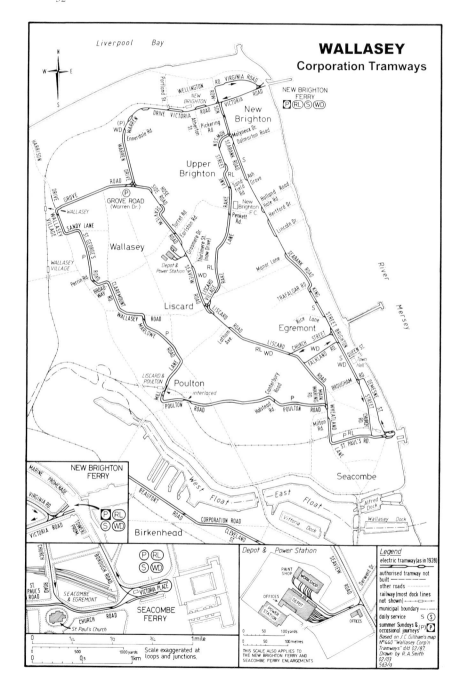

WALLASEY
Corporation Tramways

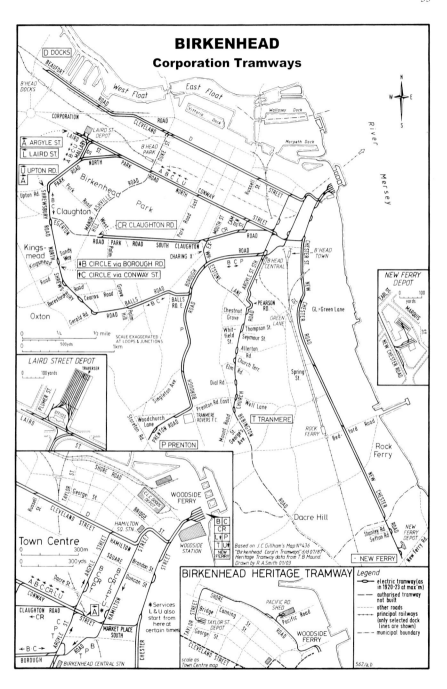

BIRKENHEAD
Corporation Tramways

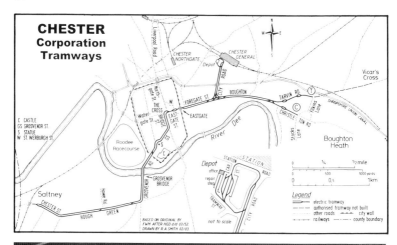

Chester purchased its demi-car, No.13, in 1906 from Brush, and is seen in the depot on 30 March 1929.

(H.Nicol, National Tramway Museum

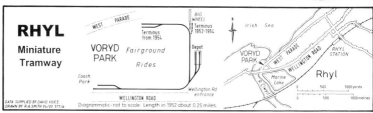

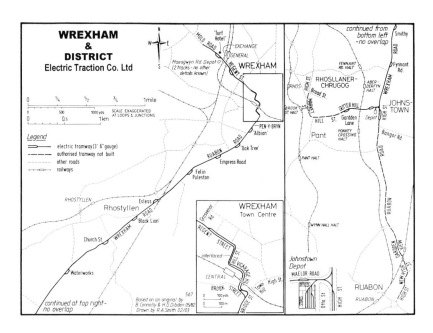

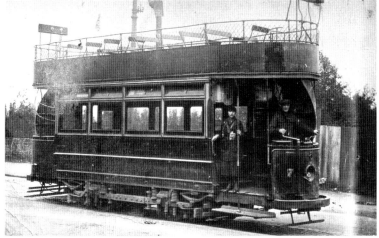

Wrexham No.7 in dilapidated condition at the northern terminus in 1929.

(E.Jones, courtesy A.W. Brotchie

SEASIDE SCENES

A well patronised Llandudno No.6 heads westwards towards town across Bodafon Fields on 8 June 1954.

(R.J.S.Wiseman

One day earlier ex-Accrington No.4 was photographed in Llandudno turning into Mostyn Street.

(R.J.S.Wiseman

One of the small Pwllheli horse trams seen on 14 September 1926

(R.L.Jones, courtesy National Tramway Museum

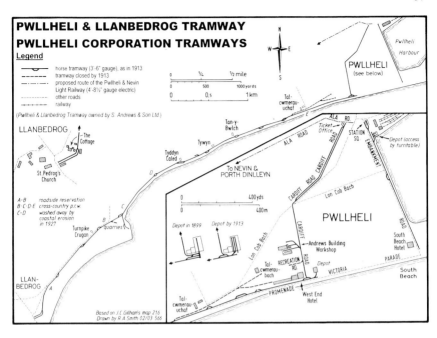

PWLLHELI & LLANBEDROG TRAMWAY
PWLLHELI CORPORATION TRAMWAYS
Legend

horse tramway (3'-6" gauge), as in 1913
tramway closed by 1913
proposed route of the Pwllheli & Nevin
Light Railway (4'-8½" gauge electric)
other roads
railway

(Pwllheli & Llanbedrog Tramway owned by S. Andrews & Son Ltd.)

N
W   E
S

Pwllheli
Harbour

PWLLHELI
(see below)

Tal-
cwmerau-
uchaf

LLANBEDROG

The Cottage

Tan-y-
Bwlch

Tywyn

Tyddyn
Caled

To NEVIN &
PORT DINLLEYN

ALA RD.

Ticket
Office

ALA   ROAD

STATION
SQ.

Depot (access
by turntable)

EMBANKMENT

St. Pedrog's
Church

A-B   roadside reservation
B-C-D-E cross-country p.r.w.
C-D   washed away by
       coastal erosion
       in 1927

Turnpike
Crugan

Quarries

C

B

Lon Cob Bach

PWLLHELI

CARDIFF ROAD
CARDIFF

CARDIFF ROAD

0   400 yds
0   400 m

ROAD

South
Beach
Hotel

Depot in 1899   Depot by 1913

Andrews Building
Workshop

Lon Cob Bach

Tal-
cwmerau-
bach

RECREATION
RD.

Depot

VICTORIA

PARADE

South
Beach

LLAN-
BEDROG

A

Tal-
cwmerau-
uchaf

PROMENADE

West End
Hotel

West End
Hotel

0   ¼   ½ mile
0   500   1000 yards
0   0.5   1 km

Based on J.C. Gillham's map 216
Drawn by R.A. Smith 02/03 566

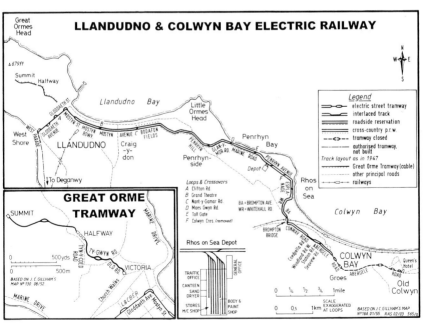

LLANDUDNO & COLWYN BAY ELECTRIC RAILWAY

Great
Ormes
Head

△679ft

Summit
Halfway

Llandudno   Bay

Little
Ormes
Head

Penrhyn
Bay

N
W   E
S

Legend

electric street tramway
interlaced track
roadside reservation
cross-country p.r.w.
tramway closed
authorised tramway,
not built
Track layout as in 1947
Great Orme Tramway (cable)
other principal roads
railways

West
Shore

LLANDUDNO

GLODDAETH ST.
MOSTYN ST.
GLODDAETH AVENUE
MOSTYN ST.
BODWY
MOSTYN
AVENUE
BODAFON
FIELDS

Craig
-y-
don

PENRHYN HILL
GLAN-Y-MOR RD.
MARINE ROAD
PENRHYN AVENUE

Penrhyn
side

Depot

Rhos
on
Sea

Colwyn   Bay

To Deganwy

Loops & Crossovers
A Clifton Rd
B Grand Theatre
C Nant-y-Gamar Rd.
D Maes Gwyn Rd.
E Toll Gate
F Colwyn Cres. (removed)

BA = BROMPTON AVE.
WR = WHITEHALL RD.

BROMPTON
BRIDGE

BA

CONWAY ROAD

Coedgelli Rd.
Woodlands Rd.
Station Rd.
Seaview Rd.
ABERGELE

Queen's
Hotel

COLWYN
BAY

Groes

ABERGELE   ROAD

Old
Colwyn

GREAT ORME
TRAMWAY

SUMMIT

HALFWAY

MARINE   DRIVE

TY-GWYN RD.
TWY-N-COED
ROAD
OLD RD.

VICTORIA

Church Walks

MARINE   DRIVE

L & B EBER

Gloddaeth Ave.
Mostyn St.

Rhos on Sea Depot

TRAFFIC
OFFICE

CANTEEN
SAND
DRYER

STORES
M/C SHOP

GENERAL
OFFICE

BODY &
PAINT
SHOP

0   500 yds
0   500 m

BASED ON J.C. GILLHAM'S
MAP Nº 130 08/52

0   ¼   ½   ¾   1 mile
0   0.5   1 km

SCALE
EXAGGERATED
AT LOOPS

BASED ON J.C. GILLHAM'S MAP
Nº186 01/55 RAS 02/03 565/a

Tramcar Fleet Lists

All cars were four-wheel double-deck unless otherwise stated.

Seating figures shown 22/34 for lower and upper decks respectively.

The opening dates shown are the first day of regular public service.

The closing dates given for horse and steam operated tramways is the day the service closed, in many cases under a different operator. For electric services it is the last full day of public service.

Birkdale and Southport Tramways Company

See page 65

Birkenhead Street Railway Co. Ltd.

4.05 miles,5ft.2in.gauge,from 1864 4ft.8½ in, Horse traction. Opened 30 August 1860. Livery light green. Purchased by the Birkenhead Tramways Company 1877. Initial fleet Nos.1-2, double-deck seating 24/24; Nos.3-4,single-deck,seating 24,. They were imported from the USA and assembled by Robert Main, Canning Street, Birkenhead.Nos.5-8, single-deck,imported from the United States in 1861.

Hoylake & Birkenhead Rail & Tramway Company

2.38 miles, 4ft. 8½ in. gauge ,Horse Traction. Opened 6 September 1873. Livery maroon. Purchased by the Birkenhead Tramways Company on 12 October 1879. Fleet details:- Nos. 1-8 double-deck, Starbuck,1873.

Birkenhead Tramways Company

8.07 miles, 4ft. 8½ in. gauge, Horse Traction. Formed in 1877, ran the above companies until 1889 when the lines were purchased by the Birkenhead Corporation and leased to the new Birkenhead United Tramways,Omnibus and Carriage Co. Ltd. Fleet details:- 1-8(ii) 1876 Starbuck, double-deck, seating 22/24. varnished mahogany and scarlet red livery. No.7, and probably others sold to Birkdale and Southport Tramways Company c1888. Nos.9-16, Starbuck 1878 double-deck cars seating 20/20; Nos.17-24 ex-Hoylake; 18(ii) plus four other small double-one-horse deck cars by G.F.Milnes in 1887. In July 1889, 27 cars, 17 in use, 10 out of use passed to the Birkenhead United.

Birkenhead United, Tramways Omnibus & Carriage Co. Ltd.

10.82 miles, 4ft.8½ in. gauge, Horse Traction. Operated the B.T.C. lines (above) ,formally from 15 August 1890 until acquired by Birkenhead Corporation in 1901. Last horse tram 8 November 1901 .Fleet details:- 27 cars ex-BTC, plus 10 short double-deck cars, seating 18/22 from G.F.Milnes in 1890, including Nos.2,5,12.

Birkenhead Corporation No.10 at new Ferry terminus. 12 September 1913.

(National Tramway Museum

Birkenhead Corporation Tramways.

13.70 miles, 4ft.8½ in. gauge, opened 4 February 1901, closed 17 July 1937. Livery maroon and pale cream.

Car Numbers	Type (as built)	Year Built	Builder	Seats	Truck(s)	Motors	Controllers
1-13 (a)	Single-deck	1901	Milnes	28+3	Peckham 14D3 MxT bogies	GE 52 6T 2 x 20hp	BTH B3
14-44 (b)	Open Top	1901	Milnes	22/33	Peckham Cantilever 9A	GE 52 6T 2 x 20hp	BTH B3
45-59 (c)	Open top	1902	Milnes	30/45	McGuire EqW bogies	E&H 11b 4 x 20hp	E&H
60-62 (d)	Works cars	1902	BCT	-	Peckham Cantilever 9A	GE 52 6T 2 x 20hp	BTH B3
63-68 (e)	Enclosed unvestibuled	1913	Hurst Nelson	28/34	HN Swing bolster MxT bogies	Siemens 250 CT 2 x 40hp	Siemens TA2

Notes

(a) Three compartment saloon cars; in 1903 partitions removed and seating increased to 30 with 3 on rear platform. Trucks replaced in 1907 by Mountain & Gibson type 3L swing-bolster, maximum traction bogies. Rebuilt 1908-10 as low bridge double-deck cars, No.1 at Laird Street, the others by Milne Voss. Seating 30/34, knifeboard on the top deck. Later fitted 28hp GE58 6T motors; BTH B3 controllers later replaced or altered to type B18.

(b) Nos. 16-17 received 'White", Great Grimsby design, enclosed balcony top covers in 1903; Nos. 14-15, 18-23, 38, 41 received Brush 'Bellamy 'covers in 1910-13; Nos. 37, 39-40, 42-44, top covered in 1914 and Nos. 24-36, seating 22/35, in 1922-3 at the Laird Street works. In 1920 Nos. 15, 19, 20, 22-24, 26, 28-30, 34, 36-37, 40-44 fitted 21E trucks, ten built by Brush. One car fitted 35hp GE58 4T in 1901. In the 1920's all re-equipped with 40hp GE 200K or BTH 200KK motors. Controllers were replaced by 1929 on Nos. 23, 38-40 by BTH B18 and on Nos. 14-22, 27, 29-33, 36-37 and 41-44 by BTH 510. No.20 now restored in open top condition..

(c) No.46, and possibly two others, cut down to single-deck in 1903 and restored to open top in 1913. All others fitted 'White' enclosed balcony top covers, seats 30/46, in 1904-5. No.50 shortened and mounted on a Peckham Cantilever 9A truck in 1910, seating 24/38. About 1923 it was re-equipped with BTH 40hp 200KK motors and BTH controllers. In 1907-8 all, except No.50, were retrucked on Peckham 14B type cantilever bogies made in Laird Street. No.49 fitted with M&G Maximum traction bogies in 1915. It is possible that Nos. 45, 48 retained their original trucks. Original Belgiam motors replaced by four 20hp GE 52 6T type in 1919-20, By 1929 Nos. 51-59 said to have had second-hand Westinghouse 90 controllers.

(d) No.60 was an ex-horse car converted in 1902 as a snowplough and later as a corrugation car. BTH B18 controllers fitted 1924.
No.61 was a water car; No. 62, another ex-horse car, was equipped as a breakdown car. It may have had a BTH R28(?) controller. When No. 60 became the breakdown car No.62 was converted back as a horse car for the 1927 Jubilee celebrations.

(e) Lowbridge cars with knifeboard seats on the upper deck.

Wirral Tramway Company horse tram No. 9 outside the New Ferry depot..

(Martin Jenkins Collection.

Wirral Tramway Company Ltd.

2.99 miles, 4ft. 8½in. gauge, Horse Traction. Opened 28 March 1877. Closed 8 May 1900 ,Livery not known. Operation taken over by Birkenhead United pending electrification. This operated from 16 May 1900 until 22 January 1901 using five ex-Wirral cars, including Nos. 4,8,9. Initial fleet Nos. 1-7, single-deck by Starbuck seating 18 plus two on each platform. They were probably sold to Wallasey in 1879 and relaced by larger Starbuck cars, believed Nos. 1-7(ii), seating 22 plus two on each platform, Nos.8-9, also from Starbuck followed in 1880. Nos. 10-13, believed G.F.Milnes, double-deck, 1894-6, seating 42, probably 20/22.

Chester Tramways Company

2.37 miles, 4ft. 8½ in. gauge, Horse traction. Opened 10 June 1879. Livery crimson lake and cream. Operation taken over by Chester Corporation from 1 January 1902. Last horse tram ran 27 December 1902. Livery crimson lake and cream. Initial rolling stock was eight small double-deck Eades reversible cars with knifeboard seats on the top tarbuck. These were replaced by eight locally built lighter cars, and one by Milnes. Two further cars bought from tarbuck. Latterly most cars fitted with garden seats. Compressed air traction trials took place in 1886 with car No. 9 cutdown to single-deck.

Chester Corporation Tramways

3.58 miles, 3ft. 6in. gauge, opened 6 April1903, closed 15 February 1930. Livery apple green and cream.

Car number	Type (as built)	Year built	Builder	Seats	Trucks	Motors	Controllers
1-12	Open top uncanopied	1903	Milnes	20/23	Brill 21E	BTH GE58 6T 2 x 28hp	BTH B18
13	Single-deck demi-car	1906	Brush	20	Brush	Brush Special	Raworth
14-18	Open top Uncanopied	1907	UEC	20/23	Brill 21E	Brush 1002B 2 x 25hp	BTH B18

Liverpool Road and Rail Omnibus Company. Old Swan Tramway

1.30 miles, 4ft. 8½in. gauge. Horse traction. Opened 2 July 1861, closed late in 1861 or early 1862. The single track was removed in the Summer of 1862. The double-deck tram was built by the Oldbury Carriage Works.

Liverpool Tramways Company Ltd.

6.88 miles, 4ft. 8½in. gauge. Horse traction. Opened 1 November 1869. Amalgamated with the Liverpool Omnibus & Tramways Company in February 1876 to form the Liverpool United Tramways & Omnibus Company Ltd.

Liverpool United Tramways & Omnibus Co.Ltd.

42.78 miles, 4ft. 8½in. gauge. Horse traction.Tramways purchased by Liverpool Corporation in 1880 and leased back. Purchased by Liverpool Corporation on 1 January 1897 and operated from 1 September 1897. Last horse tram ran 25 August 1903. Livery varied according to route. All open top double-deck cars initially by Starbuck and possibly Stephenson, later Eades reversible cars by Ashbury followed by own build at Aigburth and later Lambeth Road works. Single-ended and twin-stair cars built c1890. 331 highest numbered car; 281 cars to Liverpool Corporation. Seven cars sold to Aberdeen.

Liverpool Corporation Tramways

94.06 miles plus 4.16 worked for Bootle Corporation, 4ft. 8½ in. gauge. Opened 16 November 1898, closed 14 September 1957. Livery crimson lake and cream, from 1933 olive green and ivory; from 1950 bright green and cream. First class cars, 1908-1923, two shades of cream.

Car numbers	Type (as built)	Year built	Builder	Seats	Trucks	Motors	Controllers
400-428 (even)	Single-deck motors	1898	Busch	20	Schuckhert	Schuckhert 2 x 20hp	Schuckhert
401-429 (odd)	Single-deck trailers	1898	Busch	18	Schuckhert	-	-
432-446 (a)	Single-deck	1898	Brill	40	Brill 22E MxT bogies	Walker 35A? 2 x ?hp	Walker S7
447-458 (b)	Open top uncanopied	1899	Milnes	22/28	Peckham Cantilever	BTH GE52 2 x 25hp	DK DB1 K10
459-463 (c)	Open top uncanopied	1899	Brush	22/32	Peckham Cantilever	Westinghouse 49B 2 x 25hp	Westinghouse
464-468 (c)	Open top uncanopied	1899	Brush	22/32	Brush Peckham C	Brush 800A 2 x 17hp	Brush ?K10
469-478 (d)	Open top uncanopied	1899	ER&TCW	22/28	Brill 21E	Walker 33A 2x 25hp	Walker S1
479-484 (e)	Open top uncanopied	1899	LCT	20/26	Brill 21E	Walker 33A 2x 25hp	Walker S1

Liverpool Corporation. (continued)

Car Numbers	Type (as built)	Year Built	Builder	Seats	Truck(s)	Motors	Controllers
From September 1899 to early 1900 the above cars ,Nos. 432-458, 469-478, 459-463, 479-484 were renumbered 6-53 respectively in a new series from 1.							
54-133 141 (f)	Open top uncanopied	1899 -1900	ER&TCW	22/28	Brill 21E	Walker 33S 2 x 25hp	Walker S1
134-140 (g)	Open top -1902	1899	LCT	22/34	Brill 21E	Walker 33S 2 x 25hp	Walker S1
5 (h)	Open top	1900	LCT	24/42	Curtis	Walker 33S 2 x 25hp	Walker S1
142-441 (i)	Open top	1900-1	ER&TCW	22/34	Brill 21E	Walker 33S 2 x 25hp	Walker S1
442-447 (j)	Bellamy cover	1902-3	LCT	22/42	Brill 21E	Walker 33S 2 x 25 hp	WalkerS1
448-452 (i)	Open top	1902-3	ER&TCW	22/34	Brill 21E	Walker 33S 2 x 25hp	Walker S1
453-477 (j)	Bellamy cover	1903	ER&TCW	22/42	Brill 21E	Walker 33S 2 x 25hp	Walker S1
478-483 (j)	Bellamy cover	1902-3	LCT	22/34	Brill 21E	Walker 33S 2 x 25hp	Walker S1
1-4 (j) 484-485 492-500	Bellamy cover	1907	LCT	22/42	LCT Brill 21E	Westinghouse 200 2 x 35hp	Westinghouse 90
486-491 (j)	Bellamy cover	1907	LCT	22/42	LCT Brill 21E	DK 20 2 x 25hp	BTH B18
501-561 (k)	Bellamy cover	1908-12	LCT	22/42	LCT Brill 21E	DK 3A4 2 x 35hp	BTH B18
562-570 (l)	Bellamy cover	1908-12	LCT	22/42	LCT Brill 21E	DK20 2 x 40hp	BTH B18
571 (m)	Balcony	1912	UEC	26/40	Brill 21E	DK20 2 x 40hp	BTH B18
572 (n)	Enclosed top deck	1912	UEC	32/51	UEC Eqw.bogies	DK20 2 x 40hp	BTH B18
573-576 (l)	Bellamy cover	1913	LCT	22/42	LCT Brill 21E	DK20 2 x 40hp	BTH B18
577-599 (m)	Balcony	1913-15	LCT	26/40	Brill Radiax	DK20 2 x 40hp	BTH B18
44(ii)	Balcony	1913	LCT	22/38	Brill 21E	DK20 2 x 40hp	DK DB1 Form K3
600-605 (m)	Balcony	1919-20	LCT	24/40	Brill 21E	DK20 2 x 40hp	BTH B18
606-608 634-636 (o)	Balcony	1921	LCT	22/38	Brill 21E	DK20 2 x 40hp	BTH B18
28 cars (p)	Balcony	1920-22	LCT	22/38	Brill 21E	DK20 2 x 40hp	DK DB1 Form K
609-633	Balcony	1919-20	EE	22/42	Brill 21E	DK20 2 x 40hp	EE DK DB1 Form K3
204 cars (q)	Enclosed top deck	1922-33	LCT	22/42	Brill 21E	DK30 2 x 40hp	EE DK DB1 Form K3
637-672 674-720 733-744 (r)	Enclosed top deck	1924-27	LCT	22/42	Brill 21E	DK20 2 x 40hp	DK DB1 Form K3
721-732 745-756 673 (s)	Enclosed top deck	1927-28	LCT	23/48	Brill Radial	DK20 2 x 40hp	DK DB1 Form K3
757	Single-deck	1929	EE	44	EE EqW bogies	EE DK 120 2 x 60hp	EE DK DB1 Form NF
758-769 (t)	Enclosed	1931-32	LCT	28/42	EE EqW bogies	EE DK131 2 x 66hp	EE DK DB1 Form K3

Liverpool Corporation Tramways. (continued)

Car Numbers	Type (as built)	Year Built	Builder	Seats	Truck(s)	Motors	Controllers
770-781 (u)	Enclosed	1933	LCT	28/42	EMB Hwt bogies	CP C190A 4 x 34hp	CW Type AJ
782-817 (v)	Enclosed Domed roof	1933-34	LCT	30/40	EMB Hwt bogies	CP 190A 4 x 34hp	CW Type AJ
818-842 (w)	Enclosed Domed roof	1935	LCT	30/40	EMB Hwt bogies	CP 190A 4 x 34hp	CW Type CTTA6
843-867 TA6 (w)	Enclosed	1935-36	LCT	30/40	EMB Lwt bogies	CP 190A 4 x 27½hp	CW Type CT
868-878 880 (x)	Enclosed streamlined	1936	LCT	34/44	EMB Hwt bogies	GEC WT181 4 x 40hp	MV EP HW
881-917 879 (x)	Enclosed streamlined	1936-7	LCT	34/44	EMB Lwt L5 bogies	GEC WT181 4 x 40hp	MV EP HW
918-942 (y)	Enclosed streamlined	1936	LCT	34/44	M&T S-L bogies	GEC WT 181 4 x 40hp	MV EP HW
943-959 (z)	Enclosed streamlined	1937	LCT	34/44	EMB Lwt bogies	GEC WT181 4 x 40hp	MV EP HW
960-992 (z)	Enclosed streamlined	1937	LCT	34/44	EMB Hwt bogies	GEC WT184A 4 x 40hp	MV EP AN
151-188 (ii)(aa)	Enclosed streamlined	1937	LCT	34/44	EMB Lwt bogies	GEC WT 181 4 x 40hp	MV EP
201-300 (ii)(bb)	Enclosed streamlined	1937-42	LCT	30/40	EMB Flexible	BTH 116 AS 2 x 60hp	DK DB1 Form K3

No.293, Liverpool's last tram, is preserved at the Seashore Trolley Museum, Kennebunkport, USA., No. 245 is preserved by Liverpool Museum, No.762 at Wirral Heritage, Birkenhead, and No.869, after service in Glasgow, is at the National Tramway Museum at Crich.

Notes

(a) Nos.6,8,12,(ex-432,434,438),rebuilt double-deck,open top in 1900-1.Seating then 40/56 in No.6;40/60 others

(b) No.21, ex-447, later 40hp DK20 motors and DB1 K3 controllers. Records suggest all may have had BTH K10 controllers at some stage.

(c) These cars were rejected and later purchased by Leeds. Their Nos. 44, 46, 55, 79 and 83.

(d) Fitted Bellamy covers 1907-8.Seating 22/30.

(e) The bodies of Nos.48-50, (ex-479-481), sold to Tynemouth in 1920, but entered service with Gateshead District. (Both BET companies). Their Nos.29, 30, 38(ii) or 29, 38(ii), 30. No.51 illuminated car, 1923.

(f) No.59 rebuilt with 'Bellamy roof' and canopies in 1903,seating 22/42, remainder top covered 1907-8, seating 22/30. Re-equipped with 40hp DK20 motors and DK K3 controllers , most by 1914.Nos.51 (?), 71, 81, 94, 97, 112 and 120 had their top covers removed for use on the Great Crosby tramway, but this never took place.

(g) Experimental cars. No. 140 had a Curtis truck. All Top covered 1907-8,seating 22/40 in three cars, 22/42 in others. The former re-equipped 35hp DK9 motors.

(h) Built single-ended but soon altered to double ended. 'Bellamy' cover fitted 1905. Retrucked Brill 21E and re-equipped 40hp DK20 motors in 1919; DK DB1 Form K3 controllers in 1924.

(i) All top covered, seating 22/42, by 1905. Most older cars were re-equipped as note h above..No.227 later renumbered 345(ii).

(j) Nos.1-4 seated 22/38. The earliest covers were canvas 'blinds' over a wooden frame,but glazed covers soon replaced them. All re-equipped 40hp DK20 motors and BTH B18 controllers. No.472 was the first electric tram to be fitted with a top cover.

(k) No.501 was the first 'Standard Top-Covered' car with solid roof,the earlier 'Bellamy' roofs having a sliding panel. Some cars seated 22/38.

(l) Nos. 575-6 were built with balcony covers. No. 570 was initially equipped with Siemens 35hp type 200 motors and TA2 controllers. Re-equipped 40hp DK20 motors in 1920 and DB1 K3 controllers in 1927. 445 'Bellamy' cars were built - Nos.1-5, 134-140, 142-570 and 573-576. In 1913 at least 25 cars had replacement balcony covers. Nos.2, 4, 504, 506, 519-532, 534, 536-9, 547-561 and 584-86 were first class seating 20/34. Of the 445 cars built 15 were rebuilt to the balcony type in 1921-22 and 86 to the 'Priestly' type in 1922-3. 21 were converted to snowploughs etc and the remaining 323 scrapped.

(m) Double staircases at each end. There were a further three seats on each platform. Nos.603-5 were built with single stairs and had DK DB1 K3 controllers. No.583 initially had a Peckham R24 radial truck, No.584 a Peckham RE1 and No.599 a Brill Radiax.In 1915 No.584 received a Brill Radiax.All latterly on Brill 21E except Nos.584,599,600 on Brill Max.Traction bogies,ex-single-deck cars of 1898,from 1925-6 to 1930. Nos.603-05 had DK DB1 K3 controllers and others later so equipped.No.595 reseated 30/36 in 1915.All converted to single-stair cars by 1924.Seating 24/42.No.588 was reconditioned in 1936 with EMB flexible axle truck and 50hp MV116 motors. All later had balconies enclosed.No.596 renumbered 61(ii).Nos.594 and 597 became snowploughs in 1948 and 1942 respectively.

(n) Centre-entrance car.

(o) No.634 later enclosed.

(p) Nos.33, 70, 103, 111, 117, 125-7, 132, 319 using original bodies, Nos.43, 122, 134, 136, 209, 212, 236, 280, 291, 322, 355, 363.rebuilt with new bodies. Also Nos.138, 179, 187, 230, 287, 321 later enclosed. Eight cars initially seated 22/42.Later fitted with K3 controllers .Nos.70(ii), 138 ,230, 287 converted to Priestly Standard. Nos.179, 187, 209, 212, 230, 236, 280, 287, 291 renumbered 117, 70, 303-4, 312, 314, 330, 332 ,335 respectively. All second car number.

(q) Priestly tandard cars, from 1928 built at the new Edge Lane Works. Nos.5, 7, 9-11, 13-32, 34-42, 45-58, 60-69, 71-102, 104-110, 112-6, 118-121, 123-4, 128-131, 133, 135, 137, 139-41, 146-7, 301, 309, 313, 315, 323 ,325, 327, 334, 336, 338-40, 342, 344, 348, 353, 356, 358-9, 367-8, 372-3, 376, 378, 380, 382-3, 385-87, 389, 391, 393 and 372, All second numbered car. All third numbered car. Also Nos.151, 154-5, 164, 168, 170, 171, 186, 192, 199, 208, 214-5, 217, 219, 221, 233, 252-3, 263, 265, 268, 271, 275-6, 281, 288, 296-7, 299 renumbered 6, 8, 12, 149, 1, 126, 111, 127, 316, 142, 302, 305-7, 310-1, 343, 317-20, 324 326, 328-9, 331, 333, 337 339 and 341 respectively. All second numbered car. The following were modernised 1935-39 and re-equipped as per note s below. Some cars 60hp MV 104 or MV116 motors. Final numbers 5, 12, 28, 31, 35, 38, 54, 81, 87-9, 91, 98, 101, 105, 114, 126, 128, 147, 305, 307, 316-8, 328-9, 334, 336, 338, 340, 342-3, 353, 367, 382, 385-6, 391, 393, 407, 420, 440, 445, 451, 454 and 459. Some cars latterly had 40hp DK20 motors and K33 controllers. No.440 had a M&T truck. Seating 20/38.

(r) Priestly standard cars. Nos.661, 663-5, 667-8, 671-2, 675, 677-84, 689-91, 693, 709-10, 713, 716, 719-20 had radial trucks. Nos.647, 679, 682, 701 seated 22/38. The majority became all-enclosed,many with improved seating, (20/38).

(s) Priestly standard cars. No. 673, built in 1925, initially had EE Type 83B motors and seated 28/48. The trucks of Nos. 745-756 were from the Kilmarnock Engineering Co. All modernised 1936-9 and equipped with EMB Flexible axle trucks, 60hp BTH 116AS motors.
No.44(ii) was the prototype Priestly standard car and a further 321 were built between 1922 and 1933, although not always numbered above.

(t) All,except Nos. 758, 763, 768, reconditioned 1938-44 on EMB Lightweight bogies and fitted 4 x 40hp DK120 or GEC WT181 motors.

(u) First cars in new livery. Known as 'Green Goddesses '. Nos. 778-81 had domed roofs. No.778 fitted DB1 K3 controllers and others had controllers modified to CT TA Type.

(v) No. 809 had EMB Lightweight bogies. No. 815 later on EMB Lightweight, No. 795 was destroyed and replaced by 818 class car on lightweight bogies.

(w) No. 819 on EE Equal-wheel bogies with DB1 K3 controllers, No. 829 fitted EMB Lightweight bogies c1954.

(x) No. 905 had CP 190A motors. Nos. 869, 871, 874-5, 877-8, 880-1, 883-7, 890-1, 893, 897, 899, 901-4 sold to Glasgow Corporation in 1954.

(y) Nos. 941-2 equipped with GEC 40hp WT184A motors. All, except No. 920, sold to Glasgow Corporation in 1953.

(z) Nos. 961-2 had 40hp GEC WT 181 motors and MV HW controllers. No. 954 had HR2 type bogies.

(aa) No. 181 had HR2 type bogies latterly.

(bb) Nos. 201-213 had 60hp MV116AS motors. Nos. 201-03 had DK B AN controllers.

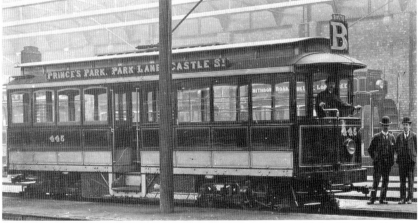

Liverpool Brill car No. 445 of 1898. *(National Tramway Museum.*

Liverpool Corporation Tramways. (continued)

Works cars

Car Type Numbers	Type	Year Re-built	Re-built	Truck(s)	Motors	Controllers
1 Lrd (a)	Stores van	1900	LCT	Curtis	BTH 2 x 25hp	Walker S1
2-3 Lrd (b)	Cash Vans	1905	LCT	Schuckhert	Schuckhert	Schuckhert
4Lrd (c)	Tow Car	1906	LCT	Schuckhert	Schuckhert	Schuckhert
408,422 (d)	Scrubbers	1907	LCT	Schuckhert	Schuckhert	Schuckhert
428 (e)	Illuminated	1902	LCT	Schuckhert	Walker 33S 2 x 25hp	DK DB1
PW5 (f)	Scrubber	1929	LCT	Brill 21E	DK 20 2 x 40hp	DK DB1 K3
- (g)	Snowbroom	1900	J.G.Brill	Brill 21E	Walker 33S 3 x 25hp	Walker S8 and 2 x Walker S1

There were also 16 salt trailers built between 1901 and 1910. These were replaced in later years by redundant passenger cars. Nos. 18(ii), 53(ii), 134, 303, 326, 376, 506-7, 513, 539, 546, 565-66 and 654 were converted for snowploughs use from 1942 to 1946.

(a) Later No. S1 on Brill 21E truck and fitted 25hp Walker 33S motors.
(b) Ex-Nos. 418, 424, later Nos, S2-3. Re-equipped trucks and motors from Nos. 44, 43 (ex-460, 459) respectively.
(c) Ex-No. 416, later No. S4. Re-equipped with truck, motors and controllers from No. 372. Acquired body of No. 569 in 1942.
(d) No. 422 received truck, motors and probably controllers from No. 298, 1921.
(e) Converted to rail-scrubber, Replaced by No.51.
(f) Lower deck of 'Bellamy' car No. 429.   (g)   Built in USA.

Liverpool and Prescot Light Railway.

3.10 miles, 4ft. 8½ in. gauge, opened 25 June 1902, transferred to Liverpool Corporation on 1 October 1919 who reconstructed the line. Closed from Long View Lane on 26 June 1949; from Page Moss Avenue on 22 June 1952 and finally from Knotty Ash on 14 September.1955. Livery dark red and cream, later green and cream. Owned by the Lancashire Light Railways Co. Ltd. Rolling stock, Nos. 37-43 and the Simplex demonstration tram, was included in the St. Helens Company fleet. See page 66.

Liverpool Overhead Railway Company - Great Crosby Tramway

2.66 miles,4ft.8½ in.gauge,opened 19 June 1900,closed 31 December 1925.Livery green and cream.

Car Numbers	Type (as built)	Year Built	Builder	Seats	Truck	Motors	Controllers
1-8 (a)	Open top uncanopied	1899	ER&TCW	22/28	Brill 21E	Walker 2 x 25hp	DK DB1
9-10	Single-deck toastrack	1899	ER&TCW	40	Brill 21E	Walker 2 x 25hp	DK DB1
11-14 (b)	Open top	1900	ER&TCW	22/36	Brill 21E	Walker 2 x 25hp	DK DB1
15-16 (c)	Open top	1903	ER&TCW	22/36	Brill 21E	??	DK DB1

Notes
Motors believed to be Walker and controllers DK DB1.
(a) Two new open top bodies purchased in 1912 were probably fitted to Nos.5 and 7. At closure Nos.2 and 4 were open top, uncanopied; No.6 open top, canopied; and Nos.1,3,5,7,8 were fitted with balcony covers.
(b) At closure Nos.12, 13 were open top, canopied; Nos.11, 14 fitted balcony covers.
(c) Both fitted balcony covers.
There were nine top covers, six from UEC, and three, probably made in the railway workshops, were fitted between 1919 and 1922.

Southport Tramways Company Ltd.

6.30 miles, 4ft.8½ in. gauge, opened 31 May 1873. Horse traction. Purchased by outport Corporation and Birkdale UDC in 1896 and leased back to the Company from 25 March 1896. Livery green and white.13 double-deck cars. Last car ran 26 March 1902.

Southport Tramways Company Ltd.

6.30 miles, 4ft.8½ in.gauge, opened 26 July 1901, Birkendale UDC absorbed into Southport Corporation on 1 January 1916. Company operation ceased on 1 March 1918 on expiry of lease. Livery green and white.

Car Numbers	Type (as built)	Year built	Builder	Seats	Truck	Motors	Controllers
1-20 (a)	Open top	1901	Brush	24/32	Brush	Brush 2 x 25hp	Brush
21 (b)	Single-deck Demi car	1903	Brush	20	Brush	Brush 800C 1 x 17hp?	Raworth

Notes
(a)   From 1903 these cars ran on one motor only.
(b)   Seats 14 in saloon plus three on each platform.

Birkdale and Southport Tramways Company.

4.05 miles, 4ft.8½ in. gauge. Horse traction. Opened 12 May 1833 .Purchased by Southport Corporation in 1900 and leased back until electrification. Livery Indian red and cream.Last horse tram ran 13 December 1902. Rolling stock included three Eades double-deck Ashbury and three single-deck Oldbury cars ex-St.Helens Tramways Company.

Southport Corporation Tramways.

17.29 miles, 4ft.8½ in.gauge, opened 18 July 1900, closed 31 December 1934. Livery maroon and cream.

Car Numbers	Type (as built)	Year built	Builder	Seats	Truck	Motors	Controllers
1-11 (a,b)	Single-deck combination	1900	ER&TCW	34	Brill 21E	DK 25A 2 x 25hp	DK DE 1 Form 1B
2-18 (c)	Open top	1900	ER&TCW	22/34	Brill 21E	DK 25A 2 x 25hp	DK DE 1 Form 1B
13 (d)	Single-deck	1900	ER&TCW	26	Brill 21E	?	?
15-17 (a)	Single-deck combination	1901	ER&TCW	34	Brill 21E	DK 25A 2 x 25hp	DK DE 1 Form 1B
20-34 (c)	Open top	1902	ER&TCW	22/34	Brill 21E	DK 25A 2 x 25hp	DK DE 1 Form 1B
21	Open toastrack	1914	ER&TCW	50	Brill 21E	DK 25A 2 x 25hp	DK DE 1 Form 1B
23,25,27 (e)	Open toastrack	1915	ER&TCW	50	Brill 21E	DK 25A 2 x 25hp	DK DE 1 Form 1B
1-17(ii) 35-44 (f)	Open top	Bought 1918	Brush	24/32	Brill 21E	DK 20A1 2 x 40hp	Brush HD 2?
29,31,33 (g)	Open toastrack	1919	ER&TCW	50	Brush	Brush 2 x 25hp	Brush
45 (h)	Single-deck saloon	1919	Southport	34?	Brill 21E	DK 25A 2 x 25hp	DK DE Form 1B

Notes
(a)   Odd numbers.
(b)   Four bodies sold to Barrow-in-Furness Corporation, 1920. Nos.1-4.
(c)   Even numbers. Eight cars fitted UEC balcony covers by 1910. Nos.8, 16, 18 re-equipped BTH B510A controllers in 1926.
(d)   Sold to Great Grimsby Street Tramways Company, 1915. No.38.
(e)   Bodies only, fitted with trucks and equipment from three of Nos.1-11.
(f)   Nos.1-17 odd numbers only. Company cars reconditioned. 12 fitted with new DK 20A1 motors. All top covered from 1920 onwards.
(g)   Equipped with trucks, motors and controllers ex-company cars 1-20.
(h)   Original combination car rebuilt for one man operation.

St.Helens and District Tramways Co.

9.01 miles, 4ft 8½ in gauge. Horse traction. Opened 5 November 1881, Rolling stock. Six Eades double-deck cars built by Ashbury, three single-deck cars by Oldbury, three double-deck cars by Metropolitan and finally one single-deck car by Milnes. Last horse tram ran in May 1890 or possibly as late as October 1893.

St.Helens and District Tramways Co. Ltd.

10.23 miles, 4ft 8½ in gauge. Steam traction. Opened 24 May 1890. Livery red. The Corporation purchased the tramways and granted a 21 year lease to the company from 1 October 1898. Transferred to the 'New 'company 1 February 1899. Last steam tram 7 April 1900.
Locomotives:-Nos.1-9 Green,1890-91.Trailers:-Nos.1-10 Milnes double-deck bogies,1890-93.

New St.Helens and District Tramways Co.Ltd.

18.85 miles, 4ft 8½ in gauge. Opened 20 July 1899, Operation transferred to St.Helens Corporation 1 October 1919. Livery maroon and white; from 1913 dark green and white. The 36 cars owned are detailed below, under the heading of St.Helens Corporation.

St.Helens Corporation Tramways

18.94 miles, 4ft.8½ in.gauge. Operated from 1 January 1919, closed 31 March 1936. Livery red and white, some cars all red.

Car Numbers	Type (as built)	Year built	Builder	Seats	Truck	Motors	Controllers
1-15 (a)	Open top Short canopy	1899	Brush	24/29	Brill 21E	GE 52-6T 2 x 20hp	BTH K10
2-16 (b)	Open top Short canopy	1899	Brush	30/37	Brill 22E	GE 52-6T 2 x 20hp	BTH K10
17-36 (c)	Open top	1900	Brush	36/43	Brill 22E	Westinghouse 46 2 x 25hp	Westinghouse 90
37-41 (d)	Open top Girder	1902	Milnes	22/35	Busch	E &H ? 2 x 25hp	
42-43 (d,e)	Open top Uncanopied	1902	BEC	22/33	BEC SB60	Westinghouse 46 2 x 25hp	Westinghouse 90
44-46 (f)	Open top	1902	Milnes	22/35	Busch Girder	E &H 2 x 25hp	?
33-36(ii) (d,g)	Open top	1918	EE	?	?	?	?
37-44(ii) (h)	Balcony	1921	Brush	22/28	Brill 21E	GE 200K 2 x 40hp	BTH
30-31(ii) (i)	Single- deck	Bought 1927	ER&TCW	54	Brill 22E	DK 3A4 2 x 35hp	DK DB Form C

Notes

Cars built in 1918 or earlier were bought from the New St.Helens &District Tramways Company Ltd. There was also an un-numbered rail grinder.

(a) Odd numbers. No.5 was reconstructed as a single-deck,one-man car in 1923. Its original Brill 21E truck was converted into a Forber 10 ft.wheelbase radial truck. 20hp GE 52 motors and EE DB1 Form K3B. controllers were fitted. (seats?) Nos.1,7,11 rebuilt enclosed in 1924-5. The latter two with top covers ex-West Riding. They had Forber radial trucks, 40hp GE 200K motors. Seating 29/46; No .7. 29/53. Nos.3 and 15 were rebuilt as balcony cars on Forber trucks in 1925. Nos.7, 9, 15 re-numbered 15, 29, 9 respectively in 1929.

(b) Even numbers. No.14 was rebuilt as a balcony car in 1924 and the bogies replaced by a Forber radial truck. Nos.2,4,6,8,10, and almost certainly Nos.12,16, fitted domed-roof balcony covers in 1921 3.No.8 and eight others 40hp BTH502FS or 502HS motors in 1925-1927. Nos.12,16 renumbered 16,12 in 1929.

(c) Soon after delivery fitted with 29hp BTH GE54 motors and BTH B18 controllers. Four cars,numbers unknown, said to have been used as trailers 1916-18. No.24 converted to works car in 1923. Nos.17-18,20-22,26-27,29,32 renumbered 30-38 respectively in 1929.

(d) Although numbered in the St.Helens fleet these cars were owned by Lancashire Light Railways Co.,Ltd. To South Lancashire Tramways in 1919.

(e) Cancelled before delivery by Aberdeen Corporation. Canopies added in 1908.

(f) Owned by South Lancashire Tramways.Loaned to St.Helens 1910-18. Other cars loaned from 1911 onwards included Nos.20,36 and 39.

(g) Equipments unknown. May have come from withdrawn cars.Renumbered 17-20.

(h) Renumbered 21-28 in 1929.

(i) Ex-Wigan Corporation Nos.68 and 77 (not necessarily in order). Built 1904. Renumbered 13-14 in 1929

Wigan Tramways Co., Ltd.

7.77 miles, 3ft.6in. gauge. Horse traction. Opened 2 August 1880. team traction 8 August 1882. Livery dark brown and cream, locomotives; dark red and cream horse trams and trailers. In receivership 1890; sold by auction 25 September 1891.

Locomotives: Nos.1-12, 1882-1887, Wilkinson; horse trams: Nos.1-8, 1880, Ashbury, Eades reversible type, open top. Nos.9-12, 1882, Starbuck open top, possibly fitted roofs for steam traction.

Wigan and District Tramways Co.,Ltd.

7.77 miles, 3ft.6in. gauge. Operated the steam tramways from October 1891; purchased by Wigan Corporation 30 September 1902 and leased back to the Company. Last steam tram 26 September 1904. Livery dark brown and cream locomotives;dark red and cream trailers.

Locomotives: Nos.1-4,7-9 ex-Nos.5-8, 10-12 of the earlier company. Nos.10-18, 1893-96, Kitson.Nos.5-6, Wilkinson, ex-Brighton and District purchased 1893. Trailers: 1-16 bogie double-deck.

Wigan Corporation Tramways.

19.23 miles plus Ince 2.85 miles, Ashton 1.99 miles and Hindley 0.45 miles.4ft .8½ in. gauge, some 3ft.6in.until 1925. Opened 25 January 1901, closed 28 March 1931. Livery crimson lake and cream, from 1913 carmine red and white. Trolleybuses replaced Martland Mill trams on 7 May 1925 and ran until 30 September 1931.

Car Numbers	Type (as built)	Year built	Builder	Seats	Trucks	Motors	Controllers
1-12 (a)	Open top	1900	ER&TCW	22/24	Peckham	Walker 33N 2 x 25hp	DK S1 or 7
13-24 (b)	Open top	1901	ER&TCW	22/24	Brill 21E	Walker 33N 2 x 25hp	DK S1 or 7
25 (c)	Works car	1902	ER&TCW	-	Brill 21E	?	?
26 (d)	Open top	1902	ER&TCW	30/32 32/32?	Brill 27G EqW bogies	?	?
27-50 (e)	Single-deck Combination	1903-4	HN	46	HN RMxT bogies	Westinghouse 200 2 x 35hp	Westinghouse 90M
51-62 (f)	Single-deck Combination	1904-5	ER&TCW	46	Brill 22E MxT bogies	Westinghouse 200 2 x 35hp	Westinghouse 90M
63-80 (g)	Single-deck	1904-5	ER&TCW	46	Brill 22E MxT bogie	DK 3A4 2 x 36hp	DK DB1 Form C
1-6(ii) (h)	Balcony	1913	UEC	30/44	Brill 43E1 RMxT bogies	DK 20A 2 x 40hp	DK DB1 Form K3
7-12(ii) (i)	Balcony	1920	EE	22/36	Preston 21E	DK 30B 2 x 40hp	DK DB1 Form K3
81-92 (i)	Balcony	1921-22	Massey	22/36	Preston 21E	DK 30B 2 x 40hp	DK DB1 Form K3
- (j)	Works car	1923	WCT	-	Brill 21E	Walker 33N?	DK S1 or 7

Notes

Nos.1-26 were built for the narrow gauge lines, the remainder for standard gauge.
(a) No.7 and later some others fitted unglazed top covers. Sold to Coventry in 1904. Their Nos.19-30.
(b) Fitted covers as above, 1903-06. New lightweight unglazed top covers fitted 1913-17, except No.24 which reverted to open top in 1919. At least four cars cut to single-deck seating 22 plus three on platforms. Also re-equipped but details not known.
(c) Details not known. Presumed van-like with revolving snow-broom.
(d) Bogies believed 27G type. Motors and electrical equipment not known.
(e) Majority, certainly Nos. 27,28,30,34,37,41,44-7,49,50, rebuilt with shortened platforms, seating 44, from 1919. No.30 had a Brill 21E truck for a time in 1922.
(f) Nos.51,54,56,57,60,61 and some others rebuilt 1921-26.
(g) Nos.63,64,67,68,75-78 and some others rebuilt 1921-26. Nos 68,77 sold to St.Helens in 1927.
(h) Sold via scrap merchant to South Shields. Nos.1,2,4,6,(ii)became Nos. 51,52 (later 33(ii)),23(ii)and 50. Others broken up for spares.
(i) Seating estimated.   (j) Built from one of the original narrow gauge cars, Nos.13-24..

Warrington Corporation Tramways.

6.84 miles,4ft. 8½ in.gauge. Opened 21 April 1902, closed 28 August 1935. Livery Munich lake and citron yellow.

Car Numbers	Type (as built)	Year built	Builder	Seats	Trucks	Motors	Controllers
1-10 (a,b)	Open top	1902	Milnes	22/33	Brill 21E	BTH GE 60 2 x 25hp	BTH K10
11-21 (a,c)	Open top	1902	Milnes	22/33	Brush A	BTH GE 60 2 x 25hp	BTH K10
22-27 (d)	Balcony	1919	Brush	22/36	Peckham P22	GE 200K 2 x 25hp	GE B18

Notes
(a) Balcony covers fitted 1905-7; Nos.1-8 Milnes Voss, 9-12 Rouse of Heckmondyke and 13-17 and 20 by McDowell a local firm.Seating 22/36. Nos. 8,9,17 and one other had balcony covers rebuilt c1924-6. Also new P22 trucks except No.17 which retained 21E as did No.19.
(b) Nos.1,2,4,5,6,10 vestibuled and fitted new Brush enclosed top covers and Peckham P22 trucks 1926-7. Seating 22/38. No.7 latterly converted back to open top condition.
(c) Brush A trucks probably replaced by Brill 21E by 1920. No.18 converted to vestibuled single-deck, one-man car 1909, seating 22 plus 6 on platforms, but later reverted to unvestibuled open-top on Brill 21E. In late 1920 's fitted balcony top cover,believed from another car.Also platform vestibules and probably a P22 truck. Nos.11,21 fitted new Brush top covers etc.as No.1,note (b)above.
(d) All latterly vestibuled,Nos.22-24,26 becoming totally enclosed.No.23 more extensively rebuilt,repanelled flush sides, c1933.

South Lancashire Tramways Company

36.96 miles including 2.85 miles Farnworth UDC, 1.97 miles Kearsley UDC and 1.40 miles Barton-upon-Irwell. In 1927-31 also 0.32 miles for Hindley UDC. 4ft. 8½ in gauge, Opened 20 October 1902, closed 16 December 1933, Farnworth lines, then worked by Bolton Corporation, closed 12 November 1944. Livery red and white.

Car Numbers	Type (as built)	Year built	Builder	Seats	Truck	Motors	Controllers
1-45 (a)	Open top	1902	Milnes	22/33	Milnes Girder	Witting 2 x 25hp	E &H
46-58 (b)	Open top	Bought 1906	Milnes	34 /40	Brill 22E MxT bogies	Westinghouse 49B 2 x 25hp	Westinghouse 90
59-82 (c)	Balcony	1906	Brush	22/36	Brill 21E	?	?
83-87 (d)	Open top	Transfer 1919	Milnes	22/33	Milnes Girder	Witting 2 x 25hp	E&H
88-89 (d)	Open top	Transfer 1919	BEC	22/33	BEC SB60	Westinghouse 46 2x 25hp	Westinghouse 90
44-45(ii) (e)	Balcony	1927	EE	34/52	EMB Burnley	GEC WT32P 2 x 50hp	EE DB1 K33E
- (f)	Single-deck saloon	1901	Milnes	20	Milnes	GE800 1 x 15hp	GE K2
-	Water car	1903	BEC	-	BEC SB 60	?	?

Notes

(a) Motors soon replaced by more powerful ones, believed 45hp. No.3 was fitted with a Milnes Voss 'Magrini' top cover for a short time c1903. 25 cars were fitted with top covers in 1914-5 and further cars were fitted with EE covers between 1919 and 1924. Seating 22/36. Nos.4, 6, 10, 38 and possibly others received new EE balcony bodies in 1920. Three cars were lent to St.Helens in 1910 for some years. Nos.20, 36, 39 also operated in St.Helens 1911-13.

(b) Ex-Farnworth Council Tramways built 1901-02. In 1923-26.Nos. 46-50, 53-58 received new EE balcony bodies and 50hp GEC WT32P motors. All except 49, 57 EMB Type A Burnley bogies, No.57 had low sideframe Burnley bogies, supplier unknown. No.49 bogies not known. Seating 34/52. Nos.47,48,50,54,55, 58 sold to Bolton in December 1933 and fitted with EE DB1 Form K controllers.

(c) The top covers were of the short roof type. Nos. 59,60,62,68,73,82 and probably others believed to have received new EE balcony covers.

(d) Nos. 37-43 in the St.Helens fleet, they were owned by Lancashire Light Railways and used, initially at least, on the Liverpool and Prescot Light Railway.

(e) New cars replacing Nos. 51-52 for Leigh-Bolton service. Sold to Bolton in 1933.

(f) Believed to be the 'Simplex' car built by Milnes in 1897 and used on the demonstration line in Prescot.

Wallasey Tramways Company.

3.31 miles, 4ft. 8½ in gauge, Horse traction. Opened 30 June 1879, Livery red and ivory. Fleet details:-Nos. 1-7, Starbuck, single-deck ex-Wirral; Nos. 8-12,Ashbury, 1880-83, double-deck Eades Patent, seating 18/20. On 8 May 1891 the tramways passed to the Wallasey United Tramway and Omnibus Company Ltd. who purchased seven double-deck cars, seating 18/16, from G.F.Milnes, Nos.6, 7, 10-14. The tramways passed to the Urban District Council on 1 April 1901 and the last horse tram ran on 19 March 1902.

Wallasey Corporation Tramways.

12.02 miles, 4ft. 8½ in gauge. Opened as Wallasey UDC Tramways,17 March 1902, closed 30 November 1933. Livery primrose green and cream, later variations dark apple green, leaf green and latterly primrose green.

Car Numbers	Type (as built)	Year built	Builder	Seats	Truck	Motors	Controllers
1-25 (a)	Open top	1902	ER&TCW	22/34	Brill 21E	DK 25A 2 x 25hp	DK DE1 Form B
26 (b)	Water car	1902	ER&TCW	-	Brill 21E	DK 25A 2 x 25hp	DK DE 1 Form B
27-31 (c)	Open top	1903	ER&TCW	22/38	Brill 21E	DK 25A 2 x 25hp	DK DE 1 Form B
32-36 (d)	Bellamy roof	1905	UEC	22/38	Brill 21E	DK 3A 2 x 36hp	DK DB 1 Form C
37-41 (e)	Bellamy roof	1907	UEC	22/38	M&G Radial	DK 3A 2 x 36hp	DK DB1 Form C
42-62 (f)	Bellamy roof	1910-13	Brush	22/38	Brush flexible axle	Brush 1204E 2 x 40hp	Brush 8B
63-68	Bellamy roof	1915	Brush	26/40	Peckham P22	Brush 1210J 2 x 45hp	Brush 8B
69-78 (g)	Bellamy roof	1920	Brush	26/42	Peckham P22	Brush 1210J 2 x 45hp	Brush 8B

Wallasey Corporation Tramways. (continued)

Notes

(a)　Top-covered, Bellamy type,by Milne Voss,1903-05, seating 33/38.

(b)　Rebuilt 1905 as a breakdown car and rail grinder.

(c)　No.27 as note (a) before entering service, Nos.28-31 later in 1903.

(d)　The DK 3A motors appear in Wallasey records as type DK 35A.

(e)　Retrucked:-　No. 41 UEC Flexible axle, 1911; No.37 Smith Pendulum, 1925; Nos. 38-40 Peckham P22, 1925-6. Motors as note (d).

(f)　Purchased in three batches:- Nos.42-51 in 1910; Nos.52-56 in 1911 and Nos. 56-62 in 1913.

(g)　Upper deck seating officially 40, but balconies seated ten rather than eight of cars 63-68. Two ex-Wallasey DE 1 Form B controllers in use on Seaton No.2.

Llandudno and Colwyn Bay Electric Railway Limited

8.38 miles, 3ft. 6in.gauge. Opened 19 October 1907, closed 24 March 1956. Livery maroon and cream; battleship grey and cream from 1914, then light green and cream from 1933.

Car Numbers	Type (as built)	Year built	Builder	Seats	Trucks	Motors	Controllers
1-14 (a)	Single deck	1907	Midland	42	M&G EqW bogies	Bruce Pebbles 4 x 30hp	BP?
15-18 (b)	Single deck Semi-convertible	1909	UEC	31	Warner Radial	Bruce Pebbles 2 x ?hp	BP?
19-22 (c)	Open toastrack	1920	EE	60	EE bogies	BTH GE249 2 x 37hp	BTH B18DD
1,3,4(ii) (d)	Single deck	Bought 1932	Brush	40	M&G EqW bogies	GE 249A 2 x 35-37hp	DK DB1 K4
2,5(ii) (d)	Single Deck	Bought 1932	Brush	40	Brush C MxT bogies	DK 30B 2 x 40hp	DK DB1 K4
6(ii) (e)	Open top	Bought 1936	UEC	30/36	Brill 22E MxT bogies	BTH GE249A 2 x 37hp	Westinghouse TIC
7-8(ii) 14-15(ii) (f)	Open top	Bought 1936	Brush	30/36	Brill 22E MxT bogies	BTH GE 249A 2 x 37hp	MV TIC
9-13(ii) (g)	Open top	Bought 1936	Brush	30/36	Brill 22E MxT bogies	BTH GE249A 2 x 37hp	BTH B49CC
23(iii) 24 (h)	Enclosed	Bought 1946	EE	24/32	EE MxT bogies	EE 305A 2 x 57hp	EE DB1 K33E
23 (i)	Single deck	Bought 1930	Brush	-	Brush	Brush 800 2 x 17hp	Brush
23(ii) (j)	Open top	Bought 1936	Milnes	-	Brill ?US type	BTH GE58 6T 2 x 28hp	BTH B18

Notes

　　　Two single-deck, single-truck 28 seat cars built by Brush for Canvey Island were used for test purposes in 1907 before the line was opened. They were returned to Brush at Loughborough. The trucks were re-used, bodies scrapped.

(a)　In 1924-5 re-equipped with 2 x 37hp BTH GE249A motors and BTH B49CC controllers.Nos.6,14,11,10 renumbered 16-19(ii)in 1936.Work on rebuilding 19(ii)as a toastrack was started but never finished.

(b)　The Warner trucks were built by Mountain and Gibson. In 1927 Peckham P35 were fitted; also 40hp BTH 502FS motors and new BTH B510 controllers. The P35 trucks, BTH Mmotors and probably the controllers were purchased by Leeds City Transport in 1942.

(c)　Mountain and Gibson type bogies. No.19 renumbered 23 for a short time in 1937, until 19(ii), retained for conversion to a toastrack was scrapped.

(d)　Ex-Accrington Nos. 28, 30, 33 and 29, 32 respectively, built 1915 (28-30) and 1921 (31-32). Nos.28, 30, 31, bought without bogies,were fitted with bogies from Nos. 1-5. Nos.2, 5 motors may have been DK11D; replaced by DK31B ex-Bradford or Manchester c1938-39. Ran in the Accrington red livery initially.

(e)　Ex-Bournemouth No.85 built 1914.

(f)　Ex-Bournemouth Nos.115-6, 121, 114 respectively. Built 1925-26.

(g)　Ex-Bournemouth Nos.108, 103, 95, 128,112 respectively,built 1921 except No.128 in 1927. No.12 controllers ex-Bournemouth 98.

(h)　All-metal centre-entrance, Ex-Darwen Nos. 24-23 respectively, built 1936-7.

(i)　Ex-Leamington and Warwick No.11, built 1901 for Taunton.Body used as a store shed from 1936.

(j)　Ex-Bournemouth No.55, ex-Poole, Nos.1-4 series built 1901. Used as a works car,latterly numbered 23A.

In 1945 the company purchased six pairs of 37hp GE249A motors ex-Birmingham Nos.97, 111, 113, 116, 137 and 207 stored since 1939 and scrapped in 1945. In 1953 about six pairs of 40hp DK 30B motors were also purchased and fitted to Nos. 6, 8, 10, 12 and 15.

No.6(ii) was preserved and is at the Southern Electric Museum,Christchurch. The Llandudno and Colwyn Bay Tramway Society own the partly restored body of No.7(ii) and have purchased that of Bournemouth No.86 for eventual restoration.

Original 1907 bogie car of the Llandudno Company.

(National Tramway Museum

Great Orme Tramways Company

1.11 miles, 3ft .6in. gauge.Cable traction. Opened 31 July 1902 to date, except closed 23 August 1932-17 May 1934, and also the upper section 7 May 2000-23 July 2001. Purchased by Llandudno UDC 1 January 1949. Livery initially deep yellow, soon Royal blue; from 1962 bright blue.

Car Numbers	Type (as built)	Year built	Builder	Seats	Trucks	
1-3	Goods Vans	1902	Hurst Nelson	-	Single truck	
4-5	Single-deck	1902	Hurst Nelson	48	bogies	Lower section.
6-7	Single-deck	1903	Hurst Nelson	48	bogies	Upper section.

Pwllheli and Llanbedrog Tramway (S.Andrew & Sons Ltd.)

3.88 miles, 3ft 0in gauge . Horse traction. Opened 1 August 1896, closed 28 October 1927. Livery dark red. Rolling stock included, possibly, 10 open toastracks seating 35 passengers on seven benches and five open trams seating 28 passengers; Also a maximum of six saloon cars seating 24 passengers. One of the open cars was fitted with a roof canopy and canvas side screens for use in wet weather. Three cars were purchased from Pwllheli Corporation in 1921.

Pwllheli Corporation Tramway

0.51 miles, 2ft.6in gauge. Horse traction. Opened 24 July 1899, closed at the end of the 1920 season, probably in September. Livery blue and white. Three, single truck cars, two open and one closed, were built by Midland Railway Carriage and Wagon Co Ltd.in 1899 and 1901. The body of the closed car has been renovated and served as an information kiosk. It is now sited at Porthmadog.

Rhyl Voryd Park Tramway

0.25 miles, 15 inch gauge. Opened 31 May 1952, closed 31 August 1957. Seasonal operation from Whitsun to the end of August. Livery green and cream.

Car Numbers	Type (as built)	Year built	Builder	Seats	Truck	Motors	Controllers
23 (a)	Enclosed Streamlined	1949	C.W.Lane	8/12	Bogies	2 x 1hp	DK type
225 (b)	Open boat	1950	C.W.Lane	18	MxT bogies	2 x 1hp	DK type
3 (c)	Open top	1952	C.W.Lane	10/10	Four-wheel	2 x 2¼ hp	DK type
6 (d)	Toastrack	1954	C.W.Lane	24	Bogies	2 x 2hp	DK type

Notes

(a) Sold in 1958 to the Scottish Tramway Museum Society, then to the Merseyside Tramway Preservation Society and now runs in a garden in South Lancashire.

(b) Moved to Eastbourne in 1954 and regauged to 2ft.Sold in 1963 to a private owner in the United States.

(c) Rebuilt slightly larger in 1953 and then as note b above.

(d) Moved to Eastbourne in 1956 and rebuilt as a 2ft. gauge open top tram. Moved to Seaton in 1974 and regauged to 2ft.9 in for operation there.

Wrexham District Tramways Company

3.31 miles, 3ft.6in.gauge. Horse traction. Opened 1 November 1876, closed 26 April 1901. Livery dark brown and cream.

No.1 single-deck toastrack, later rebuilt. No.2 open top, both by Starbuck. No.3, also open top, built locally.

Wrexham and District Electric Tramways. Ltd.

4.44 miles, 3ft.6in. gauge, opened 4 April 1903, closed 31 March 1927. Livery deep red and cream.

Car Numbers	Type (as built)	Year built	Builder	Seats	Truck (s)	Motors	Controllers
1-10	Open top	1903	Brush	20/26	Brush A	Brush 1000A 2 x 35hp	Brush B2

Wirral Heritage Tramway, Birkenhead. (Wirral Metropolitan Council)

0.60 miles, 4ft.8½in. gauge. Opened 14 April 1995. Due to be extended.

Car Numbers	Type (as built)	Year built	Builder	Seats	Truck (s)	Motors	Controllers
2 (a)	Double-deck	1882	Milnes	30/32	-	-	-
7 (b)	Open top	1876	Starbuck	22/24	-	-	-
20 (c)	Open top	1901	Milnes	22/29	Brill 21E	Ex-Barcelona	DK DB1
43 (d)	Open top	1890	LCT	24/20	-	-	-
46 (e)	Single-deck	1908	Milnes Voss	40	-	-	-
69-70 (f)	Enclosed	1992	Hong Kong	23/27	21E	EE 305C 2 x 33hp	EE DB1
78 (g)	Bellamy roof	1920	Brush	26/42	21E	Ex-Lisbon	DK DB1
762 (h)	Enclosed	1931	EE	28/42	EE bogies		EE DB1

Notes

(a) Ex-Dundee steam trailer. In store.   (b) Ex-Birkenhead horse tram.   (c) Ex-Birkenhead.
(d) Ex-Liverpool horse tram.   (e) Ex-Douglas Corporation horse tram. Red livery.
(f) First ran in Blackpool. Maroon livery.   (g) Ex-Wallasey
(h) Ex-Liverpool.Used as a pavilion in Newsham Park, Liverpool.Bogies ex-Blackpool.

Llandudno No.11 on the coast at Penrhyn Bay 7 June 1954.

(R.J.S. Wiseman

Key to abbreviations and manufacturers

Ashbury	-	The Ashbury Railway Carriage and Iron Co. Ltd., Manchester.
BCT	-	Birkenhead Corporation Tramways, Laird Street, Birkenhead.
BEC	-	The British Electric Car Co.Ltd., Trafford Park, Manchester.
Bellamy	-	Top cover named after the Liverpool General Manager.
Brill	-	The J.G.Brill Company, Inc., Philadelphia, USA
BP	-	Bruce Peebles &Co.Ltd., East Pilton Works, Edinburgh.
Brush	-	The Brush Electrical Engineering Co.Ltd., Loughborough.
BTH	-	The British Thomson-Houston Company Ltd., Rugby.
Busch	-	W.C.F.Busch, Eimsbuttel, Hamburg, Germany.
CP	-	Crompton Parkinson &Co.Ltd., Traction Division, Chelmsford.
Curtis	-	Curtis Truck Company, Decatur, Illinois, USA.
CW	-	Crompton West controllers by Allen West, Brighton.
DK	-	Dick,Kerr &Co.Ltd., Preston. Lancashire.
Eades	-	Reversible horse tram named after the Manchester Car Works Manager.
E &H	-	Compagnie Électriqué et Hydraulique, Charleroi, Belgium.
EE	-	English Electric Co.Ltd., Preston, Lancashire.
EMB	-	The Electro-Mechanical Brake Co. Ltd., West Bromwich, Staffs.
EP	-	Electro-pneumatic control.
Eq.W	-	Equal-wheel bogies.
ER&TCW	-	The Electric Railway &Tramway Carriage Works Ltd. Preston.
GE	-	The General Electric Company Inc. Schenectady, NY, USA.
GEC	-	The General Electric Co.Ltd., Witton Works, Birmingham.
Green	-	Thomas Green &Sons Ltd., Smithfield, Leeds.
HN	-	Hurst Nelson &Company Ltd., Motherwell, Scotland.
Hughes	-	Henry Hughes &Co., Falcon Works, Loughborough.
Hwt	-	Heavyweight bogies.
Kilmarnock	-	Kilmarnock Engineering Company, Kilmarnock, Scotland.
Lane	-	C.W.Lane, Modern Electric Tramways, New Barnet, Herts.
LCT	-	Liverpool Corporation Transport, Edge Lane Works, Liverpool.
LCCT	-	London County Council Tramways, Charlton Works.
Lwt	-	Lightweight bogies.
McGuire	-	McGuire Manufacturing Co., Ltd., Bury, Lancashire.
Massey	-	Massey Brothers Ltd., Wigan, Lancashire.
Metropolitan	-	Metropolitan Carriage &Wagon Co., Ltd., Saltley, Birmingham.
Midland	-	Midland Railway Carriage &Wagon Co., Ltd, Shrewsbury, later Birmingham.
Milnes	-	Geo.F.Milnes &Co.Ltd., Birkenhead also at Hadley, Shropshire.
Milnes Voss	-	G.C.Milnes Voss &Co., Ltd., Birkenhead.
M &G	-	Mountain &Gibson Ltd., Bury, Lancashire.
M &T	-	Maley &Taunton Ltd. Wednesbury, Staffordshire.
MV	-	Metropolitan Vickers Electrical Co.Ltd. Trafford Park, Manchester.
MxT	-	Maximum Traction bogies.
Oldbury	-	Oldbury Railway Carriage &Wagon Co., Ltd., Oldbury, Worcs.
Peckham	-	Peckham Truck &Engineering Co., Ltd. USA.
Raworth	-	Raworth 's Traction Patents Ltd., Manchester and Westminster.
RMxT	-	Reversed Maximum Traction bogies.
Schuckhert	-	Equipments supplied to Busch for Liverpool in 1898.
Siemens	-	Siemens Brothers Dynamo Works Ltd., Stafford.
S-L	-	Swing-link truck.
Starbuck	-	Starbuck Car &Wagon Co.Ltd., Birkenhead.
Stephenson	-	Stephenson Carriage &Wagon Co. Inc., New York, USA.
UEC	-	The United Electric Car Company,Ltd., Preston, Lancs.
Walker	-	The Walker Electric Company, Cleveland, Ohio, USA.
Warner	-	Radial truck designed by J.S.Warner; manufactured by M&G.
WCT	-	Wigan Corporation Tramways, Melverley Street, Wigan. Lancs.
Westinghouse	-	Westinghouse Electric Co.Ltd. Trafford Park,Manchester.
Witting	-	Witting, Eborall &Co.Ltd., Westminster,London.

The Electric Railway &Tramway Carriage Works Ltd.(renamed United Electric Car Company Ltd.from 25 September 1905) was a subsidiary of Dick, Kerr &Co.Ltd. which merged with other electrical companies on 14 December 1918 to form the English Electric Company Ltd. The Company also had works at Bradford, Rugby and Stafford. Most post-1908 Peckham trucks were made by the Brush Electrical Engineering Co.Ltd., and also by HN, EE and EMB. Metropolitan-Vickers were successors to British Westinghouse.

Acknowledgements and Sources

This book is based on chapters 2 and 11 of *Great British Tramway Networks* by
W.H.Bett and J.C Gillham (Fourth Edition, LRTL 1962), with additional information from recent
books, especially *Liverpool Transport* by J.B.Horne and T.B. Maund, and articles in *Tramway
Review*. Other periodicals consulted have included *The BET Gazette, Light Railway and Tramway
Journal, Modern Tramway, Modern Transport, Railway Magazine, Tramway and Railway World*.

Thanks are due to Rosie Thacker, Librarian, and Glyn Wilton, Photographic Officer, at
the National Tramway Museum, Crich, for their help with source material and for locating
photographs. Thanks are also due to M. Crabtree, F. P. Groves, P. R. Jackson, M .Jenkins, T.B.
Maund, A.R. Phillips and D. Voice for additional information.

The tramcar fleet lists have been compiled by R. J. S. Wiseman with the valued
assistance of J. Clough, E. Gahan, F .P .Groves, T. B. Maund, M. Mercer, A. R. Phillips, A. Ralphs
and D. Voice. The publishers will be pleased to receive any additional information, and this will be
published in *Tramway Review*. The maps have been drawn by R. A. Smith and are based on those
originally drawn by E. K. Stretch for South Lancashire, St. Helens and Wigan, by J. B. Horne and J.
Maher for Liverpool, and by J. C. Gillham for Birkenhead, Wallasey, Crewe, Llandudno and
Pwllheli. The area map is based on that by J. C. Gillham.

Photographs have been reproduced by kind permission of R. Brook, A. W. Brotchie,
Martin Jenkins, A. K. Kirby, Charles Roberts, the late W. J. Wyse, The Online Transport Archive,
Science Museum, Science and Society Picture Library, London, The Tramway Museum Society.

Bibliography - General

Great British Tramway Networks, by W.H.Bett and J.C.Gillham. (Light Railway Transport League,
4th. Edition, 1962).
The Definite Guide to Trams (including funiculars) in the British Isles, by David Voice. (Adam
Gordon, 2001).
The Directory of British Tramways, by Keith Turner. (Patrick Stephens, 1996).
North Wales Tramways, by Keith Turner, (David & Charles, 1979)
A Regional History of the Railways of Great Britian, Volume 10, The North West, by Geoffrey Holt,
(David & Charles, 1978) *Volume 11, The North and Mid Wales,* by Peter E Baughan. (David &
Charles, 1991)
What Colour Was That Tram? by David Voice, (Author 4th. Edition, 1998).

Atherton
The South Lancashire Tramways by E.K.Stretch, (Manchester Transport Museum Society, 1977)

Birkenhead
Birkenhead Electric Trams 1901-1937 by Charles Rycroft, (Eaton Press Ltd., Wallasey, 1993.)
The Tramways of Birkenhead and Wallasey by T.B.Maund and M. Jenkins, (L.R.T.A. 1987).

Chester
Chester Tramways by Dennis Gill and H.G.Dibdin, (in Tramway Review Nos.7,11, 1955)

Great Crosby
Great Crosby Tramways by T.B.Maund, (in Tramway Review No.171, 1991).

Liverpool
Liverpool Transport, Volume 1. 1830-1900, by J.B.Horne and T.B.Maund. (L.R.T.A., 1976).
Liverpool Transport, Volume 2. 1900-1930, Volume 3, 1931-1939, by J.B.Horne and T.B.Maund.
(Transport Publishing Company and L.R.T.A., 1982, 1987).
Liverpool Transport, Volume 4. 1939-1957, by J.B.Horne and T.B.Maund. (Transport Publishing
Company, 1989).
A Nostalgic look at Liverpool's Trams, by Steve Palmer and Brian Martin, (Silver Link Publishing,
1996).

Llandudno

The Llandudno & Colwyn Bay Electric Railway by Keith Turner, (Oakwood Press, 1993).
Tramways in Llandudno and Colwyn Bay by R. Lawson and G.C.J.Morris, (in *Modern Tramway*, Nos. 206-07, February-March, 1955).
A Nostalgic Look at Llandudno and Colwyn Bay Trams since 1945, by Geoff Price, (Silver link Publishing, 1997).

Prescot

Liverpool and Prescot Light Railway by T.B.Maund, (in Tramway Review, Nos. 165-166, (L.R.T.A. 1997).
The Simplex Car by C.C.Hall, (in Tramway Review No.131, 1987).

Rhyl

Modern Trams on 15 inch Gauge, (in *Modern Tramway*, No.195, March 1954).

St.Helens

The Tramways of St.Helens by T.B.Maund and M.J.Ashton, (in *Tramway Review*, Nos.178-180, 183, 1999-2000).

Southport

The Tramways of Southport by H.B.Priestley, (in *Tramway Review*, Nos.124-125,1985-86). Wallasey *The Tramways of Birkenhead and Wallasey* by T.B.Maund and M. Jenkins. (L.R.T.A. 1987).

Warrington

The Tramways of Warrington by Roy Brook and Ron Phillips, (in *Tramway Review* Nos.172-175, 1997-98).

Wigan

The Tramways of Wigan by E.K.Stretch, (Manchester Transport Museum Society, 1977).

Wrexham

The Tramways of Wrexham and District, by H.G.Dibdin, (in *Tramway Review*, Nos.116-117).

IN LIVERPOOL
THE FUTURE IS BRIGHT

Nos.220, 216 at Gillmoss. 11 August 1955.   *(R.J.S.Wiseman*

Inside Back Cover
Above: Great Orme No.4 at the Halfway Station at the top of the lower section on 31 March 1993.
(R.J.S.Wiseman)
Below: Llandudno and Colwyn Bay Toastrack No.21, with an ex-Bournemouth car behind, at West Shore terminus, Llandudno, on 17 June 1951.   *(W.J.Wyse, LRTA London Area)*

Published 2003 by the Light Rail Transit Association, 13A The Precinct, Broxbourne, Herts. EN10 7HY. Printed by W. J. Ray, Spectrum House, Leamore Lane, Walsall WS2 7DQ. Tel.: (01922) 428267.